How to Succeed
in Community Service

How to Succeed

in Community Service

BY DONALD AND KEITH MONROE

J. B. LIPPINCOTT COMPANY

PHILADELPHIA AND NEW YORK

First Edition

Contents

Warning: Read This First

PLEASE don't try to apply every precept in this book to every voluntary group. That way lies madness. You'll read and use this book more comfortably if you draw a line in your mind between the two great classes of civic-betterment organizations. You probably belong to some of both, and can see fundamental differences between them.

One class might be labeled the clubs. This includes the organizations which make fraternizing and socializing a big part of their program, yet plunge into assorted community projects as other major items in their routine. The service clubs, for example— Rotary, Kiwanis, *et al.* The fraternal lodges such as Masons and Elks. The veterans' organizations. The younger men's groups— Junior Chamber of Commerce, 20-30 Club and the like. (The Junior Chamber, incidentally, is not an auxiliary or little brother of the Chamber of Commerce. The two organizations are quite dissimilar, and quite unrelated in most cities. The Junior Chamber is a service club for younger businessmen.) Some church clubs also fall into this category.

The other class might be called the agencies. These are organizations or committees formed to meet some specific need of people outside their own ranks. All the youth-serving movements such as Little League, YMCA, Scouts—and schools—are in this class. So are hospitals, and groups which combat various diseases: the Cancer Society, Heart Fund, and many others. So is a committee for slum clearance or a civic theater. All welfare groups are agencies in the broad sense: churches, libraries, adoption organizations, the Red Cross, the Salvation Army, even the Community Chest and the United Fund.

One fundamental difference between a club and an agency is the manner by which people are drawn into them. The clubs recruit by social ties alone, as a country club or pinochle club would; people join because their friends belong. The agencies recruit by arousing interest in the particular civic need they were organized to meet.

A club member may have only casual interest, at first, in any specific service project of the club. Therefore he's likely to find himself on committees which mean little to him. This would be unlikely in an agency. By the same token, a committee chairman in a club may be saddled with less enthusiastic committeemen than he would in an agency.

Much of this book fits both clubs and agencies. But you will see sections which apply only to one or the other. Chapter 1, for example, has little use to you when you're pondering an invitation to join a club. And obviously the chapters on coping with a professional staff don't apply to members of clubs and brotherhoods which have no such staff.

This book isn't meant to be read straight through

The book will help you, we hope, if you use it as a travel guide. Whenever you approach some particular area of civic endeavor

—heading a committee, perhaps, or raising funds—you can pick it up and read the pages describing that area. The elaborately detailed table of contents is worded to help you find the right pages.

The authors assume that you know more than they do. You are presumed to be a successful business or professional person, giving spare time to unpaid work for the public good. Your success in your vocation indicates that you know how to judge people, how to get them to work, how to measure and control results —which is what you'll do, mostly, in community affairs. This book won't attempt to add to your expert knowledge of these skills.

It will try to show how to use these skills in nonbusiness situations, working with people who are not beholden to you. There are differences between paid work and unpaid work which may jar you. On the other hand, there are similarities you may not expect.

Although the book speaks primarily to the businessman, we hope it may be of use to his wife in her own multifarious civic chores, and to the hard-pressed social worker in helping the laity see how best to lend a hand.

CHAPTER 1

Why Were You Invited?

You too can be a civic benefactor

As EVERYONE knows who has been in both, a civic enterprise seldom runs as smoothly as a business.

Nonprofit organizations are started by great-hearted people who see a need and plunge in. They seldom see how much money will be needed, how it can be raised, or how the organization can be managed. "I just say to the Lord, 'I'll do the work, and You do the worrying,' " explained one minister who successfully ran an orphanage for years on a nonexistent budget.

This is where you come in. Probably the Lord sent you.

Your administrative skill can help bring less fortunate people better health, a bigger chance in life, a brighter environment, a boost against misfortune. All such projects strike snags in finance, purchasing, personnel, public relations, logistics, methods engineering and many other fields which businessmen are best equipped to tackle.

Look around. There are plenty of chances to serve. The Internal Revenue Service lists forty thousand organizations devoted to social betterment. People are always in trouble. Reforms are always needed. New ideas and new causes (and fine old ones) beg for attention.

Down through every echelon of management. businessmen by

the thousands are lavishing time and talents on nonprofit service. They find it baffling at first: raising money for charity isn't the same as raising it in business, and unpaid workers are quite different from employees.

Nevertheless (or should we say consequently?) part-time volunteer service is an exhilarating game when you play it well. This book will try to show you the ground rules, the pitfalls, and the proved strategies.

Do they want a letter-header?

"We want you on our executive board," says your friend Peter, a director of the Society for the Preservation of something-or-other.

What's behind his invitation? Why does the society want you? Let's consider the various possible explanations.

Conceivably, Peter and the society want nothing except your name. This isn't likely—but it's possible.

The society may be one of those almost extinct organizations which cling to the old theory that "social work" must be done only by paid experts, behind a front of respectable do-nothing names on the letterhead. This theory is dying out because a dignitary-studded letterhead doesn't create the public confidence it used to.

Nevertheless, Peter may assure you that this society's board "won't require any particular time." This means either (a) they want only your name, or (b) they're afraid you'll shy from anything that looks like work, but they hope to get you interested after coaxing you onto the board.

Let's dispose of (b) first. By discreet inquiries, you can learn whether the society's board does much work. If it does, Peter hasn't been frank with you. Your proper response to his invitation is NO. You're unlikely to have a satisfactory relationship with people who think you're so lazy, or so jealous of your time, that they must trick you into sharing their load.

(Aside to any reader thinking of approaching a good potential member with this "it'll be easy" plea: You'll do better to give the man a full explanation of why his talent is needed and how much work is involved. This is more flattering. He's more likely to get interested and say YES.)

Now for (a). Inquiry may reveal that board meetings of this society occur only quarterly, and/or consist of nothing much but staff reports and entertainment. Then obviously the society wants you merely as a figurehead. If Peter is your good friend, perhaps you'll feel happy to oblige.

But first you'd better ask some basic questions, and get truthful answers. Peter may not know the truth. Do some independent checking.

Just why does the society think your name will be useful? Does it want to give contributors the impression that you guard the purse strings, making sure their money is well spent? If so, are you willing to trust the socity with your good name? Is there any inkling that its real insiders hope to defraud the public? Each year, charity racketeers put a hundred million dollars into their own pockets.

What are this society's true aims? What does it do? How does it operate? Who are its staff people and key backers? Are they skillful and upright? You need to know. Your name on the letterhead will be construed as your endorsement of the society's aims, methods, and personnel.

You may recall a few patriotic-sounding organizations which turned out to be subversive. People named on their letterheads were mortified, and in some cases it cost them more than embarrassment.

For these reasons, you'll want to look before you leap into any unfamiliar civic group. Remember, though, that an organization seeking mere letter-headers is rare today. Most welfare movements are honest to the core, and they want earnest board members. A man who expects to give only his name, while the board wants his time and talent, will eventually annoy everyone concerned—himself most of all.

Or a golden goose?

Some groups recruit a prosperous man in half-hidden hope that he will give money as well as his name—but nothing else.

If you appear to be well-heeled, your friend Peter's assurance that "this won't take any time" may be a clue that you're cast for the role of dumb, blind angel. His society may be happiest if you limit yourself to writing checks, and perhaps taking a closely guided tour of inspection when everything is prettied up for you.

If the society simply wants your money, it would be more honest to say so. There's nothing wrong with soliciting contributions to a worthy cause, and no legitimate need for camouflaging.

Therefore, be wary of signs that an organization wants to milk you in the dark. Primary among these signs is the assurance that you won't be urged to attend meetings. Perhaps there'll even be a sly hint that your active participation is unwelcome. If the group isn't that bold, it may tip its hand by putting you on the board but not on any of its working committees.

When you suspect you're slated to be a name-only board member and big donor, there are several courses open to you.

If you're willing to give money, and believe in the society's aims and personnel, you may play along. You can attend or skip meetings, go on conducted tours to see what you've bought, and perhaps delight in reading reports given you.

A second course may be better if you believe in the society but doubt the acumen of its key people. As a donor, you're in a strategic spot. You can transform yourself from golden goose into adviser and partner. Drop in unannounced for surprise inspections. At meetings, jolt everyone by objecting whenever you disapprove of what you see and hear. You needn't threaten to withdraw financial support. The threat is there, unspoken. Board and staff will jump to appease you.

A third and happier strategy, if you're fully sympathetic with the organization, is to handle yourself as you would on the directorate of a business enterprise. Attend all board meetings. Speak up when the need arises, but show enthusiasm for the cause.

This may pleasantly surprise the society. The chances are they'll welcome your contributions to their total judgment. You'll probably find yourself becoming, not a stubborn Lord Bountiful protecting your investment by threats, but a full and valued partner.

Civic groups need this kind of trustee, whether they know it or not. And civic-minded men get the most fun from this kind of service.

Or a hatchet man?

Peter and the society may have a different motive for inviting you, if you're known as an aggressive hard-nosed type.

They may want you to fight certain battles for them. Sometimes a new man—especially a new president or committee chairman—is led into a group for this sole purpose, like a lion turned loose in the arena to chew up troublesome heretics.

Before you join the fray, you'll want the facts. You may be flattered by an appeal from people who need a vigorous champion, but their side of the story isn't the only side. Who are their enemies? And why?

The society may need a duelist to win a fair allotment from the Community Chest or a square deal at City Hall. In this case you may be glad to play D'Artagnan. On the other hand, you just might be heading into a collision with the ministerial association, the Chamber of Commerce or the Parent-Teachers Association. Are you sure you're on the right side?

Another possibility: Peter and his pals may hope to crush some element within the society. You may be expected to bear the brunt of a battle to remove a staff man with a strong following, or to force out a bloc of "mossbacks" or "rebels" on the board. One man's Mede is another man's Persian. Are you sure who is which?

They probably want your talent

The traps just described aren't common now. People in welfare work are wiser than they used to be. They seldom approach anyone for stupid or devious reasons.

Highly trained social workers who once desired only to tend their flocks without meddling from "lay people" now know they can't do the job alone. They need influential spokesmen. They need expediters to help get supplies and speed up operations. They need fund-raisers. They need accountants and tax experts. They need steersmen who know the problems and points of view of the whole community. They need organizers. They need policymakers of broad background.

Consequently, when a businessman is asked into an uplift movement today he is almost always expected to put his brains into it. The era of eat-it-and-beat-it membership in service clubs and lodges is ending. And it's hard now to find any hierarchy larded with directors who don't direct.

Very well. Assuming that you're invited into the Society for the Preservation of something, and that it doesn't want you for a figurehead or hired gun, what does it want?

It wants virtually every skill used in running a business, plus some others. The major needs of every kind of volunteer service organization will be examined in detail in this book.

However, to generalize, we can say that a man is expected to use the same managerial talents in public service that he uses in business life: talent (a) in picking men, (b) in motivating them to work loyally and well, (c) in measuring and controlling results.

—and influence

But your business flair and methodology are not your only assets in civic work. Your influence is important too. Sometimes it is the biggest reason for inviting you into an organization.

You have friends. You are well connected in various quarters. Sometimes a word from you in a certain ear can make an important difference.

Any volunteer movement has to keep explaining itself, and attracting new blood. The personal example of a powerful man with powerful friends can make him a powerhouse in the movement.

Therefore you'll be expected to watch for chances to use your influence. Sometimes this means knowing whom to telephone when the group needs something. Certainly it means speaking up if the group is misunderstood or criticized by people you know. And usually it means pulling some of your friends into the swim.

Influence, yes. Pressure, no. A civic organization honestly doesn't want halfhearted recruits or grudging service. It is subtly weakened whenever anyone is high-pressured into helping. People don't work well for an organization they dislike, and they don't speak well of it.

But if you work and talk for a cause, your spark will jump to your friends. They probably are men like you, with similar talent and prestige. You can persuade some of them to join you under the association banner.

Why were you invited? Because any civic enterprise needs the abilities and influence you've shown in business. That's the most usual, the most probable explanation. If you find it is *not* the explanation, your withdrawal may be better for you and for the community.

CHAPTER 2

What's in It for You?

One would have thought that the club was a business corporation, so grimly did he occupy himself with its problems of management.

—LOUIS AUCHINCLOSS

Good men and bad choices

THE thirty-seven-and-a-half-hour week is on the way. The thirty-five-hour week, then the thirty-hour week will follow. Vacations will be longer. Leisure will be abundant. The problem will be how to use it. Indeed, this problem is already visible.

Statistics show us a variety of changes the New Leisure has brought. People travel more, yet spend more time at home. More boats, more books, more garden tools, are sold. Church membership has shot up. The number of symphony orchestras has doubled in a decade.

As you find yourself with more free time, how will you spend it? Your choice may be roughly predictable by the kind of work you do. Managerial men normally spend less time than do laborers and clerks enjoying TV, movies, and sports. Instead they give more of their leisure to home duties, volunteer associations, and church work, according to a study by R. Clyde White in the

American Journal of Sociology. Therefore, if you are a business or professional man, the years ahead will probably find you devoting a good share of your spare hours to various activities for the benefit of your fellow men.

What activities? Take your pick; there are scores of different ones in any community. After a little dabbling and experimenting, you may feel strongly drawn toward certain ones. Just plunge into whichever you find most satisfying. This is the only sound way to choose. (And if the organization is slow to embrace you, be patient; it is merely following sound organizational practice, for reasons which you'll see in Chapter 3.)

We all know people who measure their labors in church and civic bodies by a sly estimate of how much their business will be fattened, or how far up the social rainbow they will rise. But somehow such people are easy to spot, aren't they?

Through some mysterious law of human affairs, whoever aims at aggrandizement or applause while going through the motions of helping other people is likely to harm himself. The grandstand may cheer him a while, but people down in the arena soon take his measure.

He may talk loudly and smile warmly. He may become president or Grand Inflated Ruler. Yet nothing much happens. Since his heart isn't in what he's doing, his accomplishments are mostly for show, and they don't last. Being a bluffer, he feels insecure. After a while he fades from the picture. The Bible and the classics are sprinkled with warnings to him: "Give thyself with thine alms . . . do good by stealth . . . seek first the kingdom of God." The worth of such seemingly unworldly advice is evident every day in civic affairs.

The real if invisible rewards go to the man who pitches in without self-interest. He gets what he sought—satisfaction at filling a need—and other benefits as well. "Leisure is not a vacancy, an escape from doing things," wrote August Heckscher, director of the Twentieth Century Fund. "Men and women have attained leisure only when they recapture in their free time something of what in their happiest moments they find in work—the satisfaction born of having mastered manageable things, the relaxation that comes from moving in an element where one feels instinctively at home."

In other words, as you become adept at your unpaid civic jobs, they become fun. Perhaps you get no applause, no gratitude, but you don't mind. The principle is the same as in any other do-it-yourself hobby or amateur sport. Your growing skill, and your results, are reward enough.

Emerson's advice, in the quaint phrases of a century ago, is still useful:

> If you would serve your brother, because it is fit for you to serve him, do not take back your words when you find that prudent people do not commend you. Adhere to your own act, and congratulate yourself if you have done something strange and extravagant and broken the monotony of a decorous age.

Black eyes while you wait

"The year Fabian was president was the year we did nothing."

"Bleaux? Talks big but doesn't produce."

"Sypher isn't much account. Comes to meetings but never does a lick."

Such remarks about a man are the penalty for mediocre work in civic affairs. He takes a serious risk if he joins because of pressure, or to please friends, or to gain personal advantage. Unless he has an intense desire to serve well, he'll probably serve poorly. Most kinds of unpaid work can't be successfully done without emotional involvement.

The biggest mistake made by men in volunteer organizations

is to think that their nonperformance will go unremarked. Through the intermingling memberships of service clubs and civic boards and fraternal orders, hundreds of people in a city know how strongly or feebly a man performs. Earnest volunteers don't forget when a cohort lets them down, and the word gets around.

A hard-pressed careerist may not think of himself as shirking when he slights an unpaid job. He may unquestionably be too busy for it (although the busiest of us seem to find time for anything we really want to do). Busy or not, failure to fulfill an accepted community chore may be a bad blunder.

Mr. Nero Fabian was one of the most successful businessmen in his city. Jovial and magnetic, he had built a prosperous air-conditioning business by hard work and high-voltage salesmanship. Naturally he was a service club member. In time he became its president.

In Mr. Fabian's philosophy, belonging to a service club was useful because he made contacts there, but he thought service projects were window dressing to dazzle the public. He let them take care of themselves.

Under his gavel the noon meetings were cheery and sparkling. But Mr. Fabian avoided the conferring and phoning and letter-writing and legwork usually done by a conscientious president. He looked good, he thought, and this was what mattered to him. Or maybe he didn't much care how he looked. His business was the big thing, and his service club was unimportant. Or so he thought.

By the time his term was over, the membership was smoldering with silent disgust. Everyone knew the club had drifted downhill for a year. Dedicated members who wanted nothing for themselves were angry because every challenging proposal had been lost in the shuffle. They were humiliated because their club was labeled as a do-little outfit. And they were contemptuous of their president. Consequently when they needed air-conditioning they called someone else. Mr. Fabian's business has never been the same since.

Mr. Joseph Bleaux was a building contractor. He was generous to his children and later his grandchildren (he believed in taking care of his own, he always said) but he loudly opposed the Community Chest and all that mush-headed sympathy for every worthless slob and charity chiseler who held out a hand.

His rantings annoyed many business people who worked hard on Chest drives. Gradually their annoyance pierced Mr. Bleaux's outer crust. So one year he amazed everyone by volunteering as a major in the Chest campaign. He said he could easily dragoon ten captains who in turn would each sign up ten workers for the drive. "I know plenty of people who'll be afraid to turn me down," he said.

This was true. He conscripted ten captains and herded them into his office for orders. They were a glum-looking platoon. Mr. Bleaux noticed this, and sympathized in his way.

"None of us like this Chest foolishness," he told them, "but it's here and we have to live with it. If we want to stay in business we can't ignore the do-gooders. There's no use griping about the quota the Chest has saddled us with. If we meet it, okay. If not, that just means the public isn't willing to give, and these charity agencies will have to economize a little and live within their income. Now, I know you're all busy men. Just go out and get as near to ten workers apiece as you can. Have them put what time they can into phoning or calling on the names they'll be given."

At report meetings during the campaign, Mr. Bleaux's promises were as orotund as those of the other majors. But when the final tally was in, none of his captains had a full team, and their collections were meager compared to others. Nobody commented to Mr. Bleaux. But everybody in the Chest organization—which comprised most of the public-spirited people in town—heard that

"Bleaux talks big but doesn't produce." Naturally the Chest didn't invite him to serve in subsequent years, and the reason was widely known.

A time came when a big hotel was to be built nearby. Bleaux Contracting Company was the logical firm to build it. But one of the investors in the hotel venture had been on the Community Chest board. "Bleaux talks big but doesn't deliver," he told his associates. So Joe Bleaux didn't get the hotel contract, or other big jobs which followed, because of the reputation he had unconsciously acquired.

Mr. Will Sypher was an eager junior in a low echelon of a corporation. His job was dull. If only he could wangle a transfer to another department, he thought, his merit would be visible.

The corporation sponsored a recreation program for employees. Each department was expected to send a representative to the recreation committee. Because Will seemed able to spare the time, his department sent him. Unfortunately, Will's sport was sailing. He also loved to watch big-league baseball. But he was bored by volleyball, bowling and other amusements promoted by the company.

One day a good job opened in another department. Will's superior suggested his name. But the chairman of the recreation committee, when queried about him, said, "Sypher isn't much account. He comes to meetings but never shows initiative."

So Sypher didn't get transferred. In unpaid work, people get a black eye by doing nothing.

This applies at all levels. The absentee board member, the inactive committeeman, the slacker in the fund drive, the backer who welshes on his pledged contribution, the coach who is chronically late for practice, the member who promises to serve but begs off—all may think their defection is unnoticed. But behind their back it is talked about and remembered.

Will the good Samaritan lose his shirt?

"Some people around my office are beginning to ask, 'Why doesn't that guy devote a little more time to the telephone company?' " reported Keith McHugh, president of the New York Telephone Company, in an interview with the *Wall Street Journal*. Nevertheless, Mr. McHugh goes on spending part of every working day and three evenings a week on a dozen assorted civic chores.

Although George Romney, president of American Motors, is on the job fifteen hours a day, he devotes Sundays and part of Saturdays to leadership of Mormon activities in Detroit. He worries whether stockholders will approve, but he keeps at it.

"Boy, you better start spending more time in the store," a Montgomery Ward executive warned a New England store manager who was strenuously involved in community toil. However, the home office of Montgomery Ward issued a directive to its stores: "All employees are encouraged to assume their fair share of civic obligations to the extent this can be done without neglecting the duties of their job."

Most of us wonder if we jeopardize our own bread and butter by taking time off to cast bread on the waters. We know we could make more money, or get ahead faster, if we shunned altruistic ventures and concentrated on Number One.

True, selfish men often make pots of money. But few of us would trade places with them, for we can guess at the curdled state of their innards. We know too that many other, happier rich men are civic-service buffs and have been since their modest beginnings.

No proof acceptable to a scientist or jurist can be cited in support of Emerson's metaphysical "law" of compensation, yet many people say their own experience confirms it:

The magnanimous know very well that they who give time, or money, or shelter to the stranger—so it be done for love and not for ostentation—do, as it were, put God under obligation to them, so perfect are the compensations of the universe. In some way the time they seem to lose is redeemed and the pains they seem to take remunerate themselves. But hospitality must be for service and not for show, or it pulls down the host.

Businessmen seldom stay in business unless they are practical and realistic. Therefore it's strange to see how widely they accept the idea that their welfare is bound up in the welfare of all. *Fortune* has reported: "The leading businessmen donate a large portion of their time to public activities for which they receive no remuneration." An American Management Association poll shows that a majority of the 202 company presidents interviewed are giving about five hours weekly to welfare projects. And these are men who haven't many hours to spare. They average an eighty-five-hour work week.

In the lower echelons, unpaid work is just as common. "Perhaps the fastest-growing element in United States public service today is the personal participation of businessmen," writes the *Wall Street Journal*. A Long Island Lighting Company survey indicates that its executives "who do not participate in community affairs are practically nonexistent." Procter & Gamble's code for company executives requires them to allot one-third of their time to unpaid civic service. At Du Pont so many employees are active that the company cautions them to "participate in, but not dominate" Delaware's civic projects. As long ago as 1930, International Business Machines exhorted its people: "Be outstanding citizens of your community. That is as important as being a good man in business."

Can so many companies and individuals be so public-spirited without sound reason?

Nevertheless, in trying to do good we get hurt sometimes. Smarting with self-pity, we are tempted to quit. In such dark hours it is heartening to read what Basil King wrote in *The Conquest of Fear* after a long series of afflictions:

> I remembered how many times the Bible begins some bit of pleading or injunction with the words, "Fear not." When, at some occasional test, dismay or self-pity took hold of me I formed a habit of saying to myself, "Go at it boldly, and you'll find unexpected forces closing round you and coming to your aid." Which is just what I did. To an amazing degree people were friendly, while conditions improved.

You are far less alone in community service than in business. Many fine people care about you. You'll be astounded to see how much they care, if and when you need them.

The strange joy of looking for trouble

"Eight years ago I thought I was the only one in the world with worries," said Leo Seligman. "Then I started thinking about other people's worries. Mine don't look serious any more."

Mr. Seligman knows a lot about trouble. His hobby is helping ex-convicts get a new start in life. He finds it so much fun that he makes seven trips a month to Tennessee prisons and penal farms, and has spent $15,000 from his own pocket to help 1,018 hard cases he has met there, although he is not a wealthy man.

Why do busy, successful people knock themselves out for charity? One answer can be found in the writings of a reputedly cynical critic and satirist, who declared that the important thing in life is to have the sense of "being used for a purpose recognized by yourself as a mighty one; the being thoroughly worn out before you are thrown on the scrap heap; the being a force of Nature instead of a feverish, selfish little clod of ailments and grievances complaining that the world will not devote itself to making you happy." Thus spake George Bernard Shaw in his preface to *Man and Superman.*

Another answer is in the simple words of an immigrant restaurateur who devotes his spare hours and dollars to the Red Cross:

"When I came to the United States everybody was good to me. But the Red Cross was the first group that made me feel at home. Know why? Because the Red Cross was the first to see that I didn't have to take help only but could also give. See? They asked me to join. They asked me to help. I was proud."

A somewhat more scientific answer comes from Harvard, where Professor Pitirim A. Sorokin set up a laboratory to study volunteers and the phenomenon of volunteering. "Libraries are full of studies of the criminal, the insane, the sinning, the stupid, the selfish," he explained, "but sociology has completely ignored the person of good will and good deeds."

His laboratory analyzed a thousand people named by various organizations as outstanding unpaid workers. He found that their volunteer service had benefited them mentally and physically. Such knight-errantry, he concluded, is "the best therapeutic method for securing peace of mind, meaningful happiness, real freedom, creative power for the giver."

Sometimes by middle age a man has gone as far as he will ever go in business, and begins torturing himself with the question, "What do I do with the rest of my life?" Like Alexander he yearns for new worlds to conquer. The many worlds of public work offer rousing challenges and fresh satisfaction. If fishing and loafing pall, volunteer enterprises can put a retired man back in circulation and on his mettle.

For years after retiring as chairman of General Foods, Clarence Francis kept an office in which he worked all week at umpteen unpaid jobs. "It's a happy way of showing your appreciation for living in this country," he said. Don Belding, former senior partner in a famed national advertising agency, now hustles around the country pushing his pet civic and patriotic projects. Such examples could be multiplied endlessly, from Herbert Hoover down to the humble clerk who conquered loneliness after his wife died by working for nothing every evening at the local Boys' Club as a beloved handicraft instructor.

This is not to say that community service is always fun. It plunges us into a sea of troubles—as you'll see in reading the rest of this book. Yet millions of Americans are irresistibly drawn toward it.

Trying to be your brother's keeper has therapeutic value if only as a counterirritant. When the rat race in your office is getting you down, work a few hours at helping some unfortunates and you'll forget the office. Winston Churchill says, "A change of trouble is as good as a vacation."

Many volunteers make a sad mistake by limiting their welfare work to the conference table. They never set eyes on the people who are their ultimate beneficiaries. This is why so many volunteer campaigners for the Community Chest, for example, are lukewarm. They feel quite differently if they venture into a few of the "institutions" and mingle with "cases" served by Chest agencies. If you want to get excited about your service to any organization, whether it's a Scout council or a missionary society or the state health commission, do some legwork at the grass roots. It will open your eyes—and your heart.

When a corporation needs a friend

Although the majority of business firms now give time, talent and money to community projects because they feel a social responsibility to do so, there are scornful dissenters.

"Advice to management to become 'more social-minded' is for children, not for corporate executives," says Ernest Dale, management consultant and professor of business administration, in his book *The Great Organizers.*

This recalls the dictum of the first Henry Ford, "Give the average man something, and you make an enemy of him." The same philosophy was expounded by executives of Rayonier, Inc., in a 1956 article in *Fortune.* "You can't buy good will," they theorized, "and Rayonier does not try. A big company can't expect to be loved. When a management gives away stockholders' money, it is the local manager, not the company, who is the hero or rather the sucker, since people really don't respect charity." According to the article, Rayonier called requests for cooperation in civic drives "polite blackmail" and exhorted its local managers not to give in. Since 1956 its policy may have changed, of course.

Why don't more companies take such a stand? Perhaps because they know that community hostility can hurt a company wherever it owns plants. This hostility can hit the company through Congressmen and state legislators. A company can be publicly accused of polluting water and air, and of hogging land. It can receive rough treatment in local taxation. If hostility seeps down to the lowest levels, vandalism can result.

Fortune commented editorially:

> Some observers, both inside and outside the company, think Rayonier's "new look" in community relations is actually little more than a revival of a fashion that was popular when mother was a girl. . . . Some executives feel that the company, if it loosened up a bit, would not be giving away the stockholders' money but would be making a wise investment in blunting community hostility.

If you ever face the problem of persuading a company to be more public-spirited, here are some facts which may help:

In certain towns along the tracks of Union Pacific, theivery and vandalism were problems. So the railroad threw manpower and money into organizing Boy Scout troops in these towns. Trouble stopped.

A Kaiser subsidiary had a plant in a town so grimy and sleazy that Kaiser's personnel bureau could not fill jobs there. So the plant executives used their managerial talents on community-service projects. They and their fellow townsmen made it a happier, brighter, cleaner town. Recruitment picked up.

Many a company knows that its reputation for civic-mindedness pays off in dollars and cents. People are more eager to work for it and do business with it. Congressmen, bankers, editors, churchmen and other influentials are more sympathetic. Its own good-will ambassadors form friendships in volunteer work which prove firmer than their country-club and expense-account alliances. 1169393

Taking a longer view, top management is coming to realize that it can operate more profitably in a healthy and stable society, and is therefore making a necessary investment when it helps to pay society's bills. If schools are to enlighten our expanding population, if churches are to keep ethics abreast of technology, if democracy is to be maintained, if international understanding is to be strengthened, if crime and disease are to be checked—in short, if the kind of life we cherish is to survive—then a continuous outpouring of private funds as well as private talent will be needed for public service. Business can't afford to drag its feet. A company which takes a public-be-damned attitude will be made aware by the public that the feeling is mutual.

For all these reasons, many companies have laid out systematic programs of public service. Ford, General Motors, International Business Machines, National Cash Register, American Telephone & Telegraph, all encourage employees to plunge into community projects. Marshall Field has a special vice-president in charge of civic affairs. Douglas Aircraft keeps several roving expediters on its payroll with instructions to spend most of their working day on welfare movements in high favor at Douglas.

The charitable donations of all United States corporations, large and small, average 2.49 per cent of net profits. Corporate gifts total 40 per cent of all Community Chest contributions and thirty-four per cent of United Fund donations. As the Dodge Manufacturing Corporation points out in its annual report, "Corporate giving reduces the burden on the stockholder. For every $48 the stockholder might give, his corporation can make a $100 tax-deductible gift at the same net cost."

A corporation's primary purpose must be to make money, not to do good. But the businessmen who consider that doing good is unnecessary are a dwindling minority.

Hothouse for junior executives

"Is it a good idea for junior executives to take an interest in charitable and civic groups?" an interviewer for *Cosmopolitan* asked Dr. Frederick Gaudet, director of the Laboratory of Psychological Studies at Stevens Institute of Technology.

"Yes," he said. "It helps develop men. Suppose a supervisor tends to rule in too authoritarian a fashion and his company feels he would be a better executive if he were more democratic. I would advise the company to get the fellow out into clubs, and to tell him to try to work for officership. He won't get an officership in a club on the basis of authoritarianism. If he has the stuff, he will learn a new type of leadership."

Finding himself in a realm where decisions can't be ordered but have to be negotiated, a young man grows canny and likable. An expert leader of volunteers is almost automatically an effective boss of hired help.

Therefore many corporations lend promising young employees to Community Chest and United Fund drives every year, and pay their salaries for as long as three months while they work full time on the drive. When Pacific Telephone & Telegraph vice-president George M. Dean, whose special hobby is Seattle's United Good Neighbor Fund, first started tapping junior executives in 1952, he got just ten men. By 1955 he got forty-eight men from thirty companies.

Companies find that civic work teaches a man to talk and think on his feet. It puts him in contact with many of the ablest executives in the city. It also puts him on display in a variety of testing situations, where the company can size him up and bring him along fast if he shows promise.

Any ambitious man-on-the-rise might give thought to civic work as a training ground and even a showcase for himself. Perhaps you are still too far down the ladder to be considered part of management, and nobody has suggested your name for a community campaign. If a cause appeals to you, and you see a way you can help, drop around to a few meetings or just drop hints. You'll probably be put to work, after a getting-acquainted period while people size you up. Fund-raising drives aren't the only opportunities, of course. If your heart pulls you toward youth activities, hospital work, church work, or cultural or fraternal organizations, any of these may bring your talents to bloom, and throw you with people worth knowing.

However, our earlier warnings should be underlined. Community betterment is a barren field for anyone who doesn't really believe in it, and work at it. Nobody will make his mark in it unless he possesses (or can develop) certain essential traits: loyalty, judgment, emotional stability, and an aptitude for getting along with many kinds of people.

There are certain civic organizations whose major aim is the development of young men. Among these are the Junior Chamber of Commerce, 20-30 Club, and the Toastmasters.

The Junior Chamber publishes valuable literature to help men learn civic leadership. Here are some nuggets from its *Leadership Training Manual* by Professor Fred Fielder of the University of Illinois:

> Election to office does not make a leader out of you—it just gives you a license to practice leadership. . . . Leadership is not a bag of tricks. It is a relationship between one person and a group of others. As soon as you have lost the leader-follower relationship—the group's trust and confidence in you —you have also lost your influence over the group. This may last a few minutes, or as long as the group lasts. . . . Why not get along well with everybody and be one of the boys? You were elected by the boys so you would *not* be one of them. You were elected to see that the boys could get some work done.
>
> Popularity and leadership have something in common. You can't be a leader if you make yourself obnoxious to your group. But there are many times when a man in a leadership position has to make up his mind whether he wants to be loved or to be effective.

If you're not familiar with the Junior Chamber, we urge you to look into it. It tries continuously to persuade business firms to sponsor memberships for some of their employees. This usually is worth while for both the company and the man.

Making up your wife's mind

A wife may frown when her husband begins giving evenings and week ends to volunteer organizations. Nevertheless, most "Scout widows" and "Knights of Columbus divorcees" supposedly neglected by their husbands are actually much happier than wives who keep hubby all to themselves.

For one thing, the man of the house is usually easier to live with when he gets into community work. A character in Edwin O'Connor's novel, *The Last Hurrah*, explains this to a wife vividly:

"You'll love it. He'll be completely changed. Just in little ways. He'll be more preoccupied. You know, with big issues. I don't know anything men like more than big issues. . . . Look at Jack. He's just about the perfect husband, but before he got interested in politics he was always fussing about little things; the food, or why the laundry put starch in his shirts. Then all of a sudden along came politics, and he began talking about the governor and the lieutenant governor instead of his shirts. It was much better."

For another thing, consider the contrast between the family life of Simon La Greed, a typical smart young operator who devotes every waking hour to pushing ahead in business, and Joe Galahad, who roams the night with the Boy Scouts or Red Cross.

The La Greeds' friends are all drawn from Companydom. Behind their smiles they stay watchful, because in company politics one never knows who is undermining whom. A raise or promotion can depend on what Mr. Big's wife thinks of Mrs. La Greed. So the La Greeds anxiously weigh everything they say and do in their spare time for its possible impact on Mr. and Mrs. Big and the other folks in the "company family."

But the Galahads mix with flavorsome characters who couldn't care less whether Joe drives the right car or lives in the right neighborhood. The Galahads do things totally unconnected with making money or making a splash. They constantly acquire congenial new acquaintances. At home the phone is always ringing. Mrs. Galahad moves in a swirl of sudden visitors and exciting talk about the biggest of Big Business: the business of helping other people. It's a strain. But her strain is pleasanter than Mrs. La Greed's.

Like Joe Galahad, you'll be wise to coax your wife into the orbit of your civic gyrations. Tell her what's going on. Ask her help.

Instead of holding committee meetings at an office, bring some of them into your parlor, and ask your wife to stick around as hostess. It might be unthinkable for her to say anything in a business conference, but it's easy and natural among community volunteers, because the community is her business as much as yours. Many a wife becomes an invaluable backstage bulwark in such theoretically all-male operations as the YMCA and the Rotary club.

If this isn't true in your own volunteer groups, you can help make it true. When you're going to a meeting in someone else's home, ask permission to take your wife along. Encourage other men to do the same.

And encourage your organization to pull in the wives regularly. Most of the big, seasoned clubs and agencies take pains to get support on the home front. They remember what Kipling said about the female of the species, and Congreve about the fury of a woman scorned. Therefore their annual meetings and other big conclaves are likely to be husband-and-wife style. They stage Christmas parties, ladies' nights, dances and picnics and other social gatherings for the sole purpose of keeping the wives acquainted and enthusiastic. They even organize women's auxiliaries, which often outshine the men at raising money and getting detail work done.

Before you take on community responsibilities, you'll want to make sure your wife realizes the new interests and new friends this can mean for her. By selling her in advance, or at least winning her good-natured consent to your participation, you'll avoid difficulties for yourself and the organization later on.

CHAPTER 3

Free Manpower: How to Find It

Beware the stranger who volunteers

THE WORD "volunteer" as used in social work may mislead a tyro. "Volunteer organizations" such as Scouting or the Red Cross aren't made up of people who walk into headquarters and volunteer.

In social-service talk any unpaid worker is a volunteer. The label distinguishes him from the "professional," who is salaried and is usually a career man in the movement.

Most volunteers in community enterprise don't offer to serve. They are invited in. They must be sought out, nursed along, and coached. Any newcomer who asks for work is suspect—or should be, at least temporarily.

Let's say the Amoeba Association is obviously in need of your help. You've long admired the Amoeba Association. So you drop in and offer to serve. Your offer is laudable—but don't be offended if the association keeps you at arm's length a while. There's a reason. And it isn't halitosis, or xenophobia.

Conversely, if you're on the Amoeba Association board or one of its committees, investigate before welcoming too warmly the kind stranger who offers to help tend amoebae or keep records. Investigate as closely as if he proposed to take your money and buy you a diamond mine.

Some scalawag may see a diamond mine for himself in the association, if its funds aren't properly safeguarded. Any nonprofit group may be wide open to petty thievery or worse unless there's a CPA in the picture. Other types of troublemaker may also take aim at the group as a tempting target.

Cranks try to join an organization in hope of making it their own vehicle. Communists sometimes get footholds by volunteering for the hardest work. More tragically, sex perverts seek youth-leadership jobs as the main chance at what they want.

Professionals in youth work try to screen volunteers closely, and are vigilant for signs that a wrong one has slipped in. However, nonprofessionals appoint the leaders of boys and girls in many movements. Sometimes leaders are hard to find. But if a group pulls in "anybody who's willing to work," the consequences can be bitter.

Therefore the YMCA and the Boy Scouts, among others, take the stand that a leader is unsuitable if he gives any grounds for suspicion. They don't assume that he's innocent until proven guilty. This is hard on the fellow with affectionate mannerisms and a heart of gold. But it can't be helped. Even a man who merely lets a youngster come alone to his home is putting himself in the suspicious class.

One YMCA camp director pitied a little fellow whose upset stomach kept him from a hike with the other boys. "I'll stay in camp so he won't be alone," he told his staff. "The rest of you lead the hike."

Next day the agency head fired him. "You didn't touch the boy, I'm sure," he told the camp director. "But you can't prove you didn't. Putting yourself in that spot shows such poor judgment that we can't let you work with boys."

So be cautious—whether you are the volunteer, or the man appointing one. Anybody handling money should keep books and have them audited for his own protection. Any check should always be signed by two people. Any adult and youngster, or any man and woman, should always have a third party present. Once gossip starts it's hard to disprove and harder to stop. It can be ruinous.

The Rule of Three is a standing order in most schools and many business offices. If the third person leaves, the other two must leave also. It's just as wise a rule anywhere in community work. Play safe.

And if you feel the urge to volunteer for community service, by all means do so. But make your offer to people who know you and can vouch for you. If this isn't possible, expect to be investigated, and cooperate fully and graciously.

Other pitfalls for manhunters

The chronic worry in community work is getting enough people to help. (This is true even in fund-raising drives, where the proved rule is, "If enough people see enough people they raise enough money.") Manpower must be continuously recruited, which takes trouble.

A would-be recruiter, experienced in business but not in social service, may fall into several errors.

1) He may fail to analyze the work, and therefore recruit the wrong workers. It seems odd that businessmen, familiar with job analysis in their own fields, should make such an obvious blunder in filling unpaid jobs, but they often do. They seem to think that anyone can do any civic work.

2) He may "make an appeal" in his service club. In response, the club sometimes drafts an unwilling recruit—perhaps as punishment for being absent when the appeal is made.

3) He may assign his own employees to the jobs, and preen himself on his business sacrifice. Occasionally this works, but

only if the employees are well qualified and get enough time off from other duties.

4) He may approach total strangers whom someone has suggested. Perhaps he even pays them, from his own pocket, for work which should be voluntary. Arizona once tried this system on a state-wide scale with Boy Scout troops, paying leaders from state funds. The results were sad.

5) He may know of a capable man but make only a feeble try, or none at all, to get him. He feels sure the man would refuse. Every community is sprinkled with men who could be dynamos in civic work, but aren't, because nobody asks them. Everyone thinks "they wouldn't consider it." No civic group should assume, without asking, that a desirable man is too big or too busy to help. Let him do his own refusing.

How to recruit a finance team

Next time you face the task of lining up a crew of solicitors for your favorite charity, remember that the key to success lies in four simple words: Get men you know.

This principle applies at the apex of a city-wide pyramid, at its base, and at all echelons between. If you're heading a metropolitan campaign, where thousands of solicitors are needed, you recruit colonels for the various areas. You ask each colonel to name five or six majors to work under him. Each major then signs up a team of captains, who recruit five or six solicitors apiece. Even the solicitors are customarily told to approach only prospects whom they know personally.

Whether you're seeking colonels or captains, you need men who are smooth and sparkling administrators. Each should know how to pep up his men, steer them, tactfully oust them if he must. Presumably you yourself are this kind of leader, or you wouldn't be asked to do this job; and you have friends of similar capabilities. Therefore recruiting within your own circle will produce a good crew.

This simple concept has been substantiated year after year. Virtually all social agencies operate on the principle that "like attracts like." They use their volunteers to recruit more volunteers, not only for finance campaigns but for their other voluntary enterprises.

The principle goes wrong only when some man thus recruited is too timid or busy to ask his own friends, and slides into one of the makeshifts described in the two preceding sections.

Knowing the principle can make your own civic work much easier. Of course you'll still have problems of follow-up after recruitment, but you needn't worry much if the recruits are your friends, and anyhow the ways of coping with such problems are discussed in Chapters 4 and 5.

How to recruit a committee

Scout Troop 7 was nearly dead. Its sponsoring committee was drawn from fathers of its Scouts. A parents' committee often works well for a youth group if—a big if—the parents are friends who see each other often outside the group. But Troop 7 dads didn't know each other, didn't know much about Scouting, and were high-pressured into serving. So their meetings were perfunctory, and their troop languished from nonsupport.

Then Ralph Brown, the chairman, tried a different tack. He recruited a new committee from his hunting and fishing pals. He chose only two at first: men he thought would find troop problems intriguing. They had no sons in Scouting, but they were intelligent and civic-minded.

This new committee of three friends saw each other so often that decisions no longer waited for "the monthly troop committee meeting." When the Scoutmaster presented a project, they pushed it along from week to week and often from day to day. Moreover, they got to talking Scouting on fishing trips which included other cronies. Some cronies got so interested they joined the committee officially. Troop 7 has flourished ever since.

This example simply points up the axiom that you should *get men you know* whenever you gather a committee or any staff of volunteers who will work under you.

As we saw in Chapter 1, your connections were probably a big reason you were asked to tackle the job. You aren't supposed to use these connections to coerce or cajole anyone into serving. Just the power of your example, as you happily thrash around in the job, will show your friends that the cause is attractive. Some of them will be moved to help—if you ask.

You also may benefit by inviting a few hand-picked juniors. If you mention your committee to a meritorious young acquaintance and he responds heartily, perhaps you should gather him in.

You'll seldom improve your committee by taking on strangers or casual acquaintances. They may have angled for the invitation. They may want to sit in your reflected glory. They may hope to beg favors. Or they may fear to offend you by refusing. Such committeemen will work ostentatiously but not well, hoping to dazzle you with footwork.

Conversely, your friends probably won't hesitate to tell you, "That's out of my line," or, "I can't afford the time right now," when this is true. Therefore you needn't fear that they begrudge the time if they do join.

There are other reasons, too, why friends are better than strangers for your committee. They understand your quirks; you understand theirs; you can all work together comfortably. You'll find them talking committee business not only at formal meetings, but when you forgather socially. It will be another agreeable bond between all of you—a shared hobby.

Officers: elect or select them?

In choosing officers, an organization needs to make sure that (a) it gets a suitable man, and (b) the membership will support him.

Elementary? Yes, but it gets more complex when you look into it. First the membership must be scanned to see who is available. Next the available candidates' qualifications must be investigated and evaluated. Finally the rank and file must get a chance to express approval or disapproval.

This whole process can occur either via election or selection, depending on the organization. Sometimes it doesn't occur at all—because of a mishandled election, or control by a clique. Then the organization is due for trouble. Officers will bungle, or rank and file support will dwindle, or both.

Among organizations which travel the election-campaign route successfully, prominent examples are the Junior Chamber of Commerce and most veterans' groups and service clubs. Should you aspire to become a local or national officer of one of these, you can succeed only through vigorous electioneering.

Here the traditional electoral process usually churns up strong and popular officers. All candidates' merits and demerits are aired orally or in print. Thus the scanning and investigating take place almost automatically. Mass approval or disapproval is registered by secret ballot.

Beware, though, of prescribing free-for-all elections for other organizations. Most volunteer groups would wreck themselves if they insisted on it.

The conditions under which the election-campaign method will work are: (a) candidates must be nerved to give and take public disparagement during the campaign; (b) the campaign must be hot enough, and long enough, for the electorate to become well informed; (c) the electorate must be interested enough to vote.

These conditions do not and cannot exist in the average volunteer group. The world of social work has a well-founded conviction that its unpaid offices must usually seek the men.

Why? Consider the tale of a typical organization we'll call the Lacuna League. Early in its life, the league found it couldn't persuade able leaders to campaign for office. "I'm not interested in a popularity contest," some potential candidates said. Others asked, "Why fight for the presidency? I don't want it that much, if at all."

To fill the power vacuum, glory hounds rushed in. Each was sole backer of his own candidacy, but promoted himself ardently. The league as a whole couldn't care less who won; it knew there were no heavyweights in the race. So balloting was apathetic and the new officers were pathetic.

"Next time, let's nominate and elect at the annual dinner," Lacuna League true-blues said, in the bliss of ignorance. "That way we'll get a better expression of majority sentiment."

So they did. There was no nominating committee; this would have been clique rule, in Lacuna League eyes. The big meeting was thrown open for nominations from the floor, somewhat in the manner of the Republican or Democratic national conventions.

Somebody nominated Colonel Joseph O. Blank, USA, retired. Many Lacuna insiders knew him for a pompous blowhard who recognized only three ways of influencing people: command them, break them, or kill them. But he was an imposing figure, had fought well at Belleau Wood, and was admired by those who hadn't worked with him.

A few really capable men declined nominations. As before, they had no wish for an office which somebody else wanted, and no taste for a public test of popularity. The only other nominees were self-launched, with no mass support.

So Colonel Blank was elected by partial acclamation. Nobody

cared to stand up in the assemblage, with the Colonel listening, and explain why his presidency would be a disaster. Frankness is seldom pushed so far in charitable organizations. So the Colonel soon bossed the league into extinction.

Such debacles were common when community work was learning its techniques. Now they are rare. Officers are usually selected, not elected. A nominating committee quietly canvasses for likely candidates, sizes them up, and submits a slate with one name for each office. The electorate then votes to accept the slate or refer it back to committee for a more popular recommendation. The latter choice, of course, is very seldom voted. Ordinarily the slate is approved steamroller-fashion.

This may sound like the Russian brand of "democratic election." Occasionally it is. The famous smoke-filled room of the political convention, and the legendary little group of kingmakers in the veterans' organizations, can be duplicated in any other organization which lets a clique control the nominating committee.

But this selection-before-election process is genuinely democratic if voters name the nominating committee. Preferably the president appoints a few members of the committee, and adds others suggested by his constituency. Sometimes the whole nominating committee is popularly elected—but a hazard here is that one sizable bloc of voters can pack the committee with its own people and name its own slate.

Fortunately a cutthroat struggle for power seldom occurs in a civic-service organization. Usually the problem is the same one which pervades all volunteer personnel work: picking good men and persuading them to serve.

It is fairly easy to find good potential candidates, but it is often hard to persuade them to stand for election even if unopposed. Nevertheless, good officers can be recruited. We'll examine the techniques in the next few pages. Onward!

Wooing the reluctant prospect

The time has come, we'll suppose, when you need a fine man for a hard job. Probably the job is not only hard but also rather thankless and inglorious, as most key community-service jobs are. Yet it is important. A mediocre man must not take it. He could ruin a valuable section of your organization.

This critical post might be the presidency or secretaryship of the organization itself. It might be the chairmanship of a fund drive. It might be Scoutmaster, or Sunday School superintendent, or candidate for the school board, or Great Books discussion leader, or director of a lodge chorus.

Such positions make elaborate demands on a man. So you're in for a long hard hunt.

The easiest part of the hunt is locating a qualified prospect. Having drawn the specifications of expertise and character, your committee can almost always uncover men who fit the specifications. The hard part is convincing the man that he should accept.

Being able, he surely is busy. His wife is pressing him to spend more leisure time with his family. His employer may begrudge him time off (even if it's only time at the telephone). His clubs, his church, his social life, make claims on week ends and evenings.

Probably a committeeman or two put the question to him straight, without much preamble: "Will you take the job?" Before the words are fairly out of their mouths, he is shaking his head. After a few more minutes of futile pleading, the committeemen give up.

They are repulsed just as fast by several other intended victims. Then at last they find a man who is easily persuaded. He probably is a broken reed or worse, but by now they're ready to snatch at straws. Joyously they sign him up and report to the organization that their quest is ended. We need not dwell on the probable melancholy sequel. (One Scout troop was led, within one year, by six different Scoutmasters—one of whom ended in a penitentiary.)

Able men aren't easily persuaded to invest their time and energy. But they *can* be persuaded.

The problem is a sales problem. Approach it in that mood, and it will not seem so baffling.

If you are a truck salesman, you never pin your hopes on one quick visit to a prospect who may buy a fleet. You know he already has trucks, probably intends to buy the same kind, or thinks there are several kinds better than yours.

Therefore you stalk him. You cultivate him. You maneuver him into watching your truck in action. You draw him into a chat about its selling points. You dwell upon the joys of ownership. You may arrange for him to use it temporarily, so that perhaps he will learn to love it.

Similarly, if you are an insurance salesman, you avoid frontal attacks. First you ease onto a friendly footing. You find ways to get acquainted with the family. When you are ready to solicit, your sales talk is artfully plotted to give the prospect no early chances to shake his head.

Both the truck salesman and the insurance agent try to arrange for the prospect to hear from mutual friends—"satisfied customers." The prospect's wife hears some good news about her stake in the project.

In "closing the sale" to a hesitant prospect, at least one call will usually be made by two men together. The truck salesman wants his prospect to meet the sales manager. The insurance agent wants him to meet an agency vice-president.

It works in business. It works in community uplift, too.

In courting your prospect for an important group-leadership job, there may be as many as seven different steps:

1) If the man is not familiar with the group you wish him to lead, contrive for him to visit a meeting or two as your guest.

Make sure he meets several friendly members during the meeting. Entice him into performing a few small tasks he will enjoy.

2) Next, three or four members of your committee make a massed approach. Avoiding the common blunder of tackling him at home or in the turmoil of his office, they take him to lunch, or perhaps arrange a small quiet dinner. There they put the proposition to him earnestly, stressing its appeal—a new hobby, warm comradeship, pride of accomplishment and leadership. They insist that an immediate answer is not expected.

3) Shortly afterward a few wives or mothers from the organization go to work on his wife. They ask if she knows that her husband is being approached, and if she realizes what a splendid thing it will be—how highly he must be thought of, and so on.

4) Very soon a posse from the rank and file—Boy Scouts, if it is a Scout troop he is asked to lead—should visit him at home and reinforce the invitation, pledging fealty and painting a picture of great days ahead under his leadership.

5) Influential personages can telephone or drop in to say how glad they are to hear that he may take the job. If possible, his employer will be one of these.

6) Experts will visit him. They will offer cooperation, coaching, or other forms of substantial help. He must be made to see that he won't be carrying the whole load. He should feel that whatever advice or support he needs will be at his elbow.

7) The big question will be popped in person, never by phone or mail. If the preliminary softening-up has been done with sincerity and finesse, the odds are about even that the prospect will say yes. If he says no, your committee goes on to the next prospect on your list.

Is all this elaborate spreading of the net too much trouble? Not if you care about the organization. Not if you really think the job calls for a high-caliber man.

Perhaps the man you want could be dragged in without all this courtship. Yet the courting will start him off with an inner glow; he is likely to stay longer and do a better job. Art and effort in your recruiting may pay dividends for years to come.

CHAPTER 4

Free Manpower: How to Manage It

You can never lead unless you lift.
—EDWARD EVERETT HALE

Getting off the ground

YOU HAVE recruited a friend, Henry J. Samson, into a committee or group which you direct. Now it behooves you to get him started.

You may be tempted to taxi him gently along the runway, assuring him, "This won't take much time." If you tell him this, he'll believe it. Mr. Samson won't give your group much time. He'll never get off the ground.

The attrition rate among newcomers in civic enterprise is heavy. One survey in Kansas City, covering thirty-eight different social agencies, showed 73 per cent of their board members attending rarely or never.

Why? You know why, if you've served on some average boards. You joined eagerly, only to find you had no apparent duties beyond attending meetings and listening passively to reports. True, this took little time. But the challenge, not the time, is what concerns any man worth his salt.

"If it's an easy job, then anybody can do it, and I won't bother," your Mr. Samson will think, the instant you tell him—or he sees —that you've hooked him for something trivial.

Only weak men are frightened to hear that a job is hard and will take time. If Mr. Samson were weak you wouldn't have re-cruited him, would you? If he thought your group unworthy of his best efforts, he wouldn't have joined.

So let him know specifically what you want him to do. Ridic-ulous as it seems, the reason many volunteers don't work is that they don't think they are expected to.

As a friend, Mr. Samson enlisted because you indicated you needed his help. Probably the organization itself hasn't ignited any deep crusading glow within him. This may come later, as he works with it. But now Samson sits in his office awaiting your instructions. He won't set to work uninstructed, any more than he would plant seeds in your garden until you pointed out where you wanted them.

Therefore we can put it down as an axiom: To get a volunteer to work, we must give him a specific task.

And a corollary: His job must be challenging. He must see why no lesser man was asked to do it.

Mr. Samson is a proud man, proud of his ability to do tough jobs. He was complimented when you asked his help. If then you say nothing further for several weeks, he will feel misled. Evidently you didn't need him much after all! His annoyance will be keener if, merely to keep him busy, you ask him to do something an office clerk could do.

Perhaps you can take a leaf from the *Operations Manual* for officers and directors of the Junior Chamber of Commerce. It says:

An "orientation" of each new member will take place whether you plan it or not. . . . Each time a new member attends a meeting, works on a project or talks with another member he becomes oriented. Without a planned orientation program to guide him, a new member's impressions may not be favorable. . . . Here are techniques which can create the right impression with the recruit:

Letters of welcome should be sent to the new member and to his boss.

A greeting committee should welcome members to each meeting.

New members should be inducted with suitable ceremony. Your induction program should be one which implies that we all are proud of being Jaycees.

*   *   *   *

Basic faults . . . are to fail to get new members assigned to an active committee quickly, to assign new members to an inactive or poorly functioning committee, or to have members without any committee assignment. . . .

When assignment has been made, the new member should be notified immediately . . . and a copy of the letter sent to the chairman. It is most important that proper safeguards are established to assure that the chairman is notified and takes action to get the new man active. Surprisingly, many members are often assigned to a committee but then never contacted by the chairman.

Fort Nonsense

George Washington knew that men must feel needed. In 1777, encamped above Morristown, his troops faced an idle winter. Washington saw foreshadows of disaffection. Grimly, he called his staff and told them a fort must be built at once. He doubled the sentries. He showed himself everywhere, urging along work on the fortifications.

The soldiers forgot their gloom and began betting when an attack would come. They labored furiously on the fort. When spring came it still was incomplete—yet Washington ordered a move.

"Move before the fort is finished?" the chief of engineers asked in amazement.

"It has served its purpose," Washington said with a twinkle. "It was only nonsense, to keep the men busy at something they thought important."

It is still known as Fort Nonsense, though building it was good sense. Keeping men involved in exciting enterprises is wise leadership. If possible each enterprise should be truly necessary and urgent. But if for a while there is nothing which needs doing, as a last resort aren't you better off building your own Fort Nonsense than letting your committee or board fall apart from idleness? Surely you'll want to get your people—especially your new people—agog somehow. Otherwise they may desert. (Of course they'll desert later anyway, if they discover that you deliberately deceived or manipulated them, even though you did it for the good of the group. So take care!)

This is not to suggest that your people should be kept humping every week, or that you should manufacture fake projects. The point is simply that any volunteer group may be demoralized by a long period of idleness, so an astute manager will confront his group, and its individual members, with challenges often enough to hold their loyalty.

Your foresight and imagination should keep you out of General Washington's dilemma. When your group has no work, you'll probably see long-range objectives which can be pointed up, dramatized, and made urgent. Or perhaps you can look around and find a short-range job which needs doing. Every community has long-range and short-range problems lying around untouched. Washington, with his vision, seldom would have needed a Fort Nonsense if he were in modern civic work.

Try a task force

You are chairman of a fifty-man standing committee within a big organization. How can you make all—or even many—of your committeemen feel needed? You can't put up one Fort Nonsense after another. Nor, presumably, can you find genuine projects big enough or numerous enough to keep such a large committee stirred up.

One possible answer is to fragment the committee into task forces, each with a specific short-term stint for the year. If this is the public relations committee of a metropolitan Boy Scout council, projects might be the summer camp promotion, the finance campaign, Boy Scout Week, annual circus or Scoutorama, Eagle Scout dinner, and such. Publicizing these events will take months of planning for each one; but none of them calls for fifty men. Each can be handled by a half-dozen qualified people working as a team.

With this approach, you might start your committee's year by going over the schedule and calling for volunteers to comprise the task forces undertaking each event. In the example cited, of public relations projects, you'll naturally want balance within each task force—rather than having most of your artists working on one event, most writers on another, and most printers on a third. So the volunteering should be watchfully compartmented. But you can assure each volunteer that once his big mission is over, he won't normally be urged to take any other major job in your committee for at least six months.

Thus your committee need convene only once or twice yearly. Yet its members won't feel forgotten. The rare meetings of the standing committee can review broad objectives, and honor task forces for completion of tasks.

There are three great advantages to this system:

1) A task force member knows he is committed only for a

definite operation which ends on a not-too-distant date. He is more likely to put his full weight into it.

2) Top experts can be recruited for a short-term sprint. They'll work hard for a period of weeks, though they'd never agree to attend year-round meetings.

3) Men in a task force have the fun of carrying a significant project from germination to termination. It's more satisfying than dabbling lightly in a variety of operations.

Theirs not to reason why?

Dr. Benvolio, chairman of a volunteer committee, was baffled. He often held committee meetings. It was his custom to open the meeting by explaining a problem, and proposing a solution. He then encouraged his committee to offer opinions and suggestions.

"Everybody seems to go along with my ideas at the meetings," he complained privately, "but nobody does much about them afterward."

Dr. Benvolio knew that face-to-face discussion is a handy tool of leadership. He knew that leaders in many fields have found that passing down instructions from Topside isn't enough, especially to volunteers. Blind obedience became unpopular long ago.

So Dr. Benvolio was right, of course, in explaining his plans and trying to prod subordinates to talk freely about them. But he went wrong in four other ways.

In the first place, psychologists find that a human being is loath to realize that fellow humans disagree with him. We all tend to think that our friends and colleagues recognize, deep down, the rightness of our views. Even when their words belie this, we may tell ourselves, "Joe doesn't really mean that. He just likes to argue."

Secondly, people often sit silent when they disagree with a leader, especially if they don't know him well. Most of Dr. Benvolio's committee were only casual acquaintances of his (remember the value of forming your committee from your friends?) and chose not to risk offending him by arguing.

Thirdly, every leader consciously or unconsciously wants support for his aims. His brain may tolerate criticism. But his heart yearns for admiration. When people poke a hole in Dr. Benvolio's plans, this disturbs him even though he sought it. He is subconsciously irked. Some of the committee see this even if he doesn't. He never voices irritation, but he shows it in subtle mannerisms. So now we've found three reasons why Dr. Benvolio was deceived about the solidity of his support.

In the fourth place, we all work harder for our own ideas. Dr. Benvolio seldom let people feel that they had any ideas. The problems were always those which he, from his eminence, sighted and brought down to them. The solutions were always his prefabrications. With little time to examine them, nobody felt deeply about either problems or solutions. So it isn't surprising that Dr. Benvolio's committee did little to implement his plans.

The moral, of course, is that to lead free manpower we must use its brainpower. This is hard. It calls for wholehearted acceptance of the purpose, not just the techniques, of group work.

Dr. Benvolio used the techniques. He invoked the great god Communication. He gathered people around him; was jolly with them; told them the facts; asked their opinions. But it wasn't enough.

Dr. Benvolio needed to cultivate an attitude of identifying himself with the end-product of group thinking, not with his own share in it. He needed to talk less and listen more. He needed also to help his group see its part in the bigger pattern, instead of merely tackling chores like a crew in an assembly line.

Industry knows that men whose jobs involve only a snippet of a great operation are more zealous if they understand the whole operation. So they are taken on tours of the plant. They are shown their finished product in action. They are told what happens because of it. Their suggestions are solicited, considered, sometimes adopted.

Government is learning that people carry out decisions better if they share in decision-making. After an Iowa nutrition expert told housewives why they should use more milk, only 16 per cent did so. But when he contrived for small undirected discussion groups to talk over the question, "Should we use more, or less, milk?" its use jumped 50 per cent.

This same philosophy can move mountains in volunteer service. Volunteers should understand the big operation and help plan their part of it.

It is risky to assume that they know much about the cause they serve, or that their ignorance doesn't matter. If you want them to work, take them up on the mountaintop and show them the real scope of the job they share. Show them problems, and make clear the importance of the problems. Or better, let them spy a problem with their own eyes and decide its importance for themselves.

Perhaps you already see (or think you see) how to solve these problems. But isn't it wiser to hold your tongue? Letting your cohorts grapple with enigmas may take longer, yet they'll be stronger for it. And if at last they ask, "Have you any suggestions?" they'll be far more receptive. Perhaps your suggestion can be so tentative and sketchy (by your own tact) that the committee will fill in the outline and think it was mainly their idea.

However, you'll sometimes need your gavel. One service club appointed a traffic safety committee and gave it a free hand in developing a program. But a committeeman prided himself on original ideas, and pushed them excitedly. He electrified some foolish colleagues and trampled wiser ones underfoot. His ideas weren't workable, but the committee adopted them rather than wrangle with him. The chairman who sat quietly through it all was later blamed for the costly fiasco of the club's traffic safety program.

Similarly, a tennis club appointed a committee to arrange matches with other clubs. Three good plans clashed in committee. Palaver went on so long that the club was left out of all neighboring clubs' schedules.

These were extreme cases. Weak leaders caused them, not any basic fallacy in the concept of volunteer participation. By and large, a policy of full explanation and deliberation works even better in voluntary enterprise than it does elsewhere, while a dictator creates even more dissidents than he does in compulsory organizations.

After you recruit a good man and give him a challenging task he understands, your best course is to say, "You know how to do this better than I. Go to it." You may need to add an explanation of any restrictions set by the organization's policies. Beyond this, the fewer mandates the better.

A church needed more parking space for its congregation. The church board cast a hopeful eye on a nearby clinic, whose parking lot was virtually empty Sundays. A man in the vestry was a friend of the doctors who ran the clinic, so he was empowered to dicker. Part of the board wanted to direct him to approach the owner of the clinic's land—but others said, "Don't tell him how to proceed. Let him go at it however he likes. Just tell him how much we can pay, and turn him loose." Luckily this faction prevailed.

No doubt the landlord would have snapped up extra money by renting the lot to the church on Sunday, even over protests of the doctors. But the uninstructed envoy went instead to the doctors, and got their permission to use the lot free if a few marked spaces were kept for them.

A town we'll call Blanksville had long been a stubborn holdout from its county Community Chest drives, although many Blanksville people benefited from Chest agencies. Finally the Chest board brought in an industrialist who lived in Blanksville, and asked him to set up campaign teams in the town. "Not if I have to do it your way," he said. The board hated to permit deviation from its well tested campaign plans, but it finally let him use his own judgment. He knew Blanksville problems and prejudices, and talked Blanksville language. His teams brought in 80 per cent of their quota the first year and topped it the second.

A Scoutmaster asked his troop committee to drum up parents' attendance at a gala meeting where he was to award badges and explain camp plans. The committee struggled with ideas for various mailing pieces, and vowed willingness to phone every family personally, but its general attitude was, "What's the use? We've tried all this before." Finally one committeeman, an advertising man, said, "Leave it to me and I'll get your parents out."

He printed tickets and handed them to the boys. "Admission to the meeting will be by ticket only," he told the boys. "No boy can take home more than two tickets."

The Scoutmaster felt betrayed. Turn people away from his meeting? But the adman knew human nature. People called up and asked for extra tickets. A crowd came.

Need we enlarge on the point? In your own office you surely value an associate with initiative. If you are a member of a law firm you don't tell partners how to try cases. If you are a company president you don't tutor your sales manager. In either case you could, perhaps, but you know how they would react. And they might just be more capable than you, at their specialties.

In community organizations a Big Daddy would scarcely be tolerated. Volunteers accept a few doses of indoctrination in policy and aims, but they seldom take orders as to how they should do specific jobs—particularly jobs at which they are skilled.

To sum up, then: Pick a capable man, make sure he understands his job and its necessary limitations, then give him a free hand while you watch from a discreet distance.

Payment without money

Men don't work well without reward, even in the noblest group endeavors.

In business, part of their reward is money but their psychological rewards are more important. In volunteer projects the psychological pay is all-important. And you must be one of the paymasters, especially to those volunteers whom you recruit.

Part of a volunteer's pay is the satisfaction of tackling and whipping a tough problem. As already noted, you rob him of this pay if you keep problems and plans to yourself.

Another part is appreciation. Your recruits probably joined up to please you. They certainly won't feel adequately rewarded unless you *are* pleased. You must show your pleasure.

A third part is trophies, of whatever kind. People love to win some tangible symbol of accomplishment. It may be a pin to wear in the lapel; a card to carry in the wallet; a certificate to hang on the wall; or merely one's name emblazoned somewhere on some honor roll. Whatever it is, most of us prize it more highly than we admit even to ourselves.

Bob Perin, a training-course leader famed for his showmanship throughout the Boy Scout movement, uses one shrewd gimmick which seems childish at first thought. He tells men at the beginning of a course that those who finish can have a silver star to paste on the cardboard name tags they wear during the course. He shows the stars, and jokes about them a moment. Then he hides them away and never mentions them again. But invariably at the end of every course fifteen or twenty sober, brainy businessmen stride up to Perin and demand their silver stars: the same ten-cent-store stars children get in Sunday School. We are all children under the skin in our yen for kudos, ribbons, scalps, notches in the belt, names in the paper. They are important pay for work done.

So pay your people. Give them a visible memento of their feat when you can—and above all show your appreciation.

Appreciation is sometimes hard to show. Unless you're an actor you can't turn it on like a light at the proper instant. In business you may perhaps be poker-faced and laconic. Yet you find ways to cultivate *esprit de corps*. You know your money can't buy loyalty or enthusiasm from employees.

You may not have reflected that people whom you direct in unpaid activities are, in a subtle sense, your employees. Shouldn't you use your skill as a management man in this situation?

Whatever morale building arts work for you at the office are likely to work among Masons, volunteer firemen, or the State Board of Regents. Every man, wherever he is, likes to be valued as a unique individual. Public appreciation feels good. Approval by a man's friends feels better. But what feels best—because it is rarest—is appreciation of the one friend for whom a special effort was made.

Blarney is no substitute for any of these. "Always be sincere—whether you mean it or not," says a comic slogan widely circulated. Its wry humor derives from our knowledge that transparent insincerity is everywhere. You detect a bogus compliment instantly; can't others detect those you dish out?

Praise, to mean much, must be discerning. A syrupy encomium for work that a man himself knows was mediocre is an insult to his intelligence.

Yet you must boost along your recruit while he still is groping and muddling. Therefore you take pains to show him you are interested in his difficulties, and confident he'll solve them. You give whatever help he seems to want and need. But you abstain from shouting, "Wonderful," or, "You're doing magnificently," until the facts justify it.

After the job is done a chairman of volunteers can't meet his payroll, so to speak, merely by cranking out form letters or certificates of commendation. Nor is it enough to arise in public and read off a list of people "entitled to the thanks of the community."

Such rites may be partial payment, if all the named people really did good work. But if you include a few who don't deserve it, you disillusion the others. You debase the coin in which you paid them.

Even when the gesture is valid and graceful, it isn't the same as your personal appreciation. Since your recruits are your friends, treat them as friends, warmly and informally. Keep in touch at every step, showing pleasure as they progress. When they leap a significant hurdle, your congratulations are in order—are almost essential, if you want to keep these people driving and striving.

Of course you dare not overdo your congratulations. You need only be genuine. Express your actual satisfaction, and stop.

You can take one additional step: tell several other friends how well your recruit is doing. He'll hear. It will be more convincing than your direct word of thanks.

As one man says, "When a chairman slaps me on the back for 'good work' I take for granted he does the same to everyone. But if I hear he's bragging on me elsewhere, I know he was really pleased."

Whom to boss—and how

Earlier in this chapter you may have sensed two holes in advice offered you. Let's turn back now, and see if the holes can be plugged.

We said, without much explanation, that there are limits to the leeway you can give a volunteer in doing a job. The advice, "Pick a capable man, then give him a free hand," assumed that your man would have horse sense as well as technical capacity. And we stipulated that any taboos in his path should be explained to him at the start.

But perhaps you wondered: "What if my recruit isn't capable of doing the job on his own? Or what if he starts doing it the wrong way?"

Important questions. From time to time, very likely, you'll be nursing along someone who can't make up his mind, or reining in a rash visionary. Leaving these people to go it alone would be silly. They need what social workers call "positive leadership." In other words, you'd better be tactfully bossy.

Voluntary organizations are strewn with people who aren't used to making decisions. Their leader should chat with them and nudge them along to a clear understanding of *his* decision. If he is a good salesman, he'll convince them he is simply crystallizing their thoughts and verbalizing their verdict.

But now we come to the chap who is all too decisive: the hotspur, blind to his lack of judgment or skill. He goes ahead full speed and damn the torpedoes.

Sometimes you really have to torpedo him. One civic group invited a big-name showman to stage part of a great spectacle in Municipal Stadium. He determined to put two thousand white pigeons into the air at the climax of a fireworks display. He was unperturbed by cost, or by possible consequences to birds and the people beneath them. The thrilling sight in his mind's eye carried him away. "I must have a free hand," he told the civic sponsors. "You don't understand theatrics."

To block him they had to carry the fight to their board of directors, so he resigned in high dudgeon. Probably nothing else could have happened. But the average hotspur can be kept on the track without incurring his enmity or summoning higher-ups. Seven principles for doing this are laid down by Nathan A. Baily, dean of American University's school of business:

1) Choose the right time and place to talk with him. Don't

argue while angry, or where people can listen who shouldn't. Later you'll have better perspective, and he may realize his own error.

2) Make your motives clear to him. Show that your chief concern is the good of the organization; that you're trying to help him serve it; that you're sure he'll do a fine job once he understands.

3) Speak pleasantly. Remember he wants to be helpful, and wants to be understood.

4) Listen. Make sure you fully understand his point of view and his reasoning. Perhaps you should restate them in your own words, and get him to agree that you've expressed them fairly. This may even correct misapprehensions of your own.

5) Be specific about your objections. Vagueness isn't diplomatic here. It will only embitter him.

6) Be specific about your proposed remedy. Better yet, have him propose his own specific remedy.

7) Remember you usually get farther by indirection than by frontal attack. Don't depend on logic alone. As Swift said, "You cannot reason a man out of something he was not reasoned into." If a man behaves illogically, appeal to his emotions.

However, the point made in the first section of this chapter applies here too: Even strong and wise administrators must be told what you want accomplished when they first set to work for you. And as long as the geography is unfamiliar to them, they'll be grateful for warning if they steer too close to pitfalls.

You're more awesome than you know

"Getting licked occasionally is good diplomacy when you're dealing with volunteer groups," Paul Ziffren once remarked.

Mr. Ziffren is a lawyer who, in his spare time, helped organize neighborhod Democratic clubs all over California, and built an enthusiastic volunteer movement which brought the national convention to Los Angeles in 1960. "After the convention-site committee tentatively chose Los Angeles, I deliberately took a beating by trying to clinch the choice immediately," he said. "They slapped me down and postponed the decision, to prove I wasn't calling the shots. Later, of course, they confirmed their tentative choice, as I thought they would. For the same reason, in 1958 I appeared before Democratic clubs which I knew would boo me for urging the endoresment of Clair Engle for Senator. These clubs were against Engle." By getting booed, Mr. Ziffren dispelled talk that he was growing too influential.

The same principle was laid down by Machiavelli: "It may at times be the highest wisdom to simulate folly."

The principle is worth considering when you manage volunteers whom you didn't recruit. So far we've been considering the guidance of manpower which you personally selected and pulled into harness. But at times you may supervise people fetched in by your recruits, your colleagues, your predecessors or superiors. There may even be people who came more or less unasked. If you're in charge of them, your position is delicate.

This conglomeration of humanity will view you with some awe and some distaste. As a stranger and a Big Shot, you're suspect.

So communication is obstructed. You'll need to take pains to make sure these cool subordinates understand you; and greater pains to make sure you understand them.

This applies at all levels, and in all sizes of groups. Many a club president is chilled by an odd sense of remoteness as soon as he assumes office; he no longer hears much of the small talk. Many a Scoutmaster gradually realizes how little is told him about incidents that might displease him, and how much is said behind his back. The parents and the troop committee (even those whom he recruited) may tell him no more than sergeants tell the new lieutenant.

Your problem is the simple, ancient one of making friends. The solution is old too, and has been stated so often it sounds trite: Be a friend. This isn't merely being friendly. Friendliness, as opposed to snobbishness, is simple good manners. The Queen of England would show friendliness to a reporter interviewing her. Being a friend is something else.

To jump the gulf to your constituents, a calculated effort is needed. The effort will be all yours. Unless and until they know you well, underlings will assume that you look down on them. Perhaps they admire you, in a detached or diffident way, but they don't try to be your friends. That would look like currying favor. Even if you are a saint, in America they won't kiss the hem of your garment. Saints are men apart. And if a supposed saint shows a trace of the sin of pride, if he looks slightly stuck up, then the silent fury of those who feel scorned will encompass him. Ask the pastor of any church.

To make friends with subordinates is to humanize yourself; to show that you realize you're no better than they are. Your verbal protestations won't accomplish this. The big boss who keeps saying that his outfit is one big happy family soon becomes a laughingstock or worse. Nor can you pretend to think that smaller fry could do your job as well as you.

If you suffer occasional minor setbacks through obvious errors of your own, and get laughed at or heckled, à la Machiavelli-Ziffren, it stirs up sympathy for you or at least dramatizes your non-superiority. People feel themselves your equal.

This equality they like to feel, and which they suspect you of slighting, is based on knowledge that they can do *some* things better than you. Just show them you recognize this, and you'll lubricate all dealings with them.

Mr. Buttermore, new chairman of a Rotary club committee, saw that an old-timer named Mr. Frost resented him. Needing Frost's cooperation in the committee, Buttermore took steps. "I hear you run a bottling plant," he told Frost. "I'm a lawyer, so I'm an ignoramus about bottling, but I've always been curious about it. Any chance of your taking me through your plant?"

Frost was delighted, naturally. During the conducted tour he showed off while Buttermore asked questions and looked fascinated. In an hour the two men were firm friends.

Another chairman went to a hostile committeeman for advice on his garden; followed the advice; and effused to others about the commiteeman's helpfulness. End of hostility.

This is about the shortest way with dissenters yet developed in American volunteer enterprise. Find fields in which they're clearly superior to you, then show recognition of their superiority. Of course if you really do feel above them, as they suspect, or if you even act uppity without feeling so, then you'll need to take yourself in hand before you can expect much cooperation.

"There is a certain element of neuroticism in all business leadership," according to Harvard's Professor B. M. Selekman, an expert in industrial relations. This may be hyperbole. But successful executives often do have a masterful mien which grates on the rank and file in a civic group. Moreover, executives are likely to think fast and talk well—to their own disadvantage among the commonalty. "He's too bright to be right," is an old saying in certain parts of the nation, and those who don't say it may yet think it subconsciously.

So the stronger and brighter you are, the colder you may find volunteers who don't know you. This isn't a book on spiritual reform. But you may wish to ponder a point made by Chester I. Barnard, former president of New Jersey Bell Telephone Company: Authority actually rests with those to whom orders are given. If the orders aren't accepted, no real authority exists. A typical executive mistake, according to Mr. Barnard, is to instruct people to do something they don't want to do and can't be forced to do.

When balky volunteers anger you, there are three simple rules which may help:

1) Listen. People you won't listen to will dislike you. But they like a leader who takes genuine interest in what they say. As you listen, pay heed not only to words but to motives and emotions.

2) Be patient. Shortness or briskness may seem like arrogance. So try not to interrupt objections or criticisms which come your way. Every carper feels better after he's said his say in full.

3) Be humorous. Laugh at your own mistakes and everybody relaxes, including you. It helps even when you're alone. In a group, friendly kidding (the unbarbed kind, of course) makes you one of the gang.

Service with a broad grin

One small point worth remembering: When you work with volunteer underlings who don't know you, they'll interpret your silence as disdain or displeasure. His Lordship's impassive face is thought either stupid, crafty, cold, or timid.

Therefore liveliness is indicated. Look interested. Smile. Nod enthusiastically when you can. Say something sympathetic and perspective if it occurs to you. Flashes of humor can be a big help. Real joviality is a major asset. If at all possible and proper, have fun!

Warmth spreads. It melts walls. Even if your geniality is a bit forced, it serves a purpose. It saves you from seeming regal. Moreover, by pretending enthusiasm you may become enthused. On the other hand, backslapping and bombast are no help even when they come naturally.

We must all decide for ourselves how much to dissemble enthusiasm. But it seems safe to say that when we feel joyless we don't lead as well as we otherwise could. At any rate, a good boss of volunteers will try hard not to seem distant. Whatever our politics, we all know that F.D.R.'s smile, and Ike's waves and grins, were powerful factors in attracting devoted followers.

Conversely, we've all known the brainy, incisive leader who plans everything minutely and pushes his plans with inhuman perfectionism. He may win wars or professional football games. But put him in charge of a United Fund financial drive, and he'll be pitiful. His meetings will consist of icy analyses of the short-comings of those hapless teams which haven't met quotas. He will talk tersely, truthfully, and caustically. Everybody will hate him, and nobody will hustle very hard to satisfy his demands.

There are happier ways to deal with benighted subordinates. Of course geniality is more than a smile and laugh. These are only outward symptoms of an attitude. Your attitude shows that you like them; that you like working with them; that you like to help if they need it. Having said as much by your manner, help them without meddling. And whatever the provocation, keep smiling.

The art of running contests

Perhaps you're familiar with contests in business—salesmen's competitions, production races and the like. Contests are also widely used to pep up unpaid workers. But there are significant differences betwen the civic contest and the business contest.

In business, a contest adds color and humor to the sober grind, but its real lure is the glitter of gold. The prizes have cash value. Moreover, the achievements of winners are known to their employers and brighten their future in the company.

But cash doesn't count in volunteer contests—or shouldn't. Volunteers are altruists. They put shoulders to a wheel for the satisfaction of helping.

People don't stay in civic work unless they enjoy it. The more they enjoy it, the harder they work and the longer they stay. This is where contests come in. An element of competition can make a civic job more exciting, and more fun.

In view of this basic difference between business and volunteer contests, do you agree that volunteers should not be offered prizes of commercial value?

Cadillacs and flights to Hawaii cost money, and people who donate money to welfare organizations want it used for welfare, not fancy prizes. The public watches how community movements spend money. When a movement looks overprosperous, words like "racket" and "politics" begin to fly.

It may be argued that money to buy prizes can do more good in an organization, by inspiring its volunteers, than the same amount spent any other way. Well-meaning donors often reason thus, and put up prizes spontaneously. But this cuts no ice with the whispering public. "If he wants to help, why doesn't he just give his money like the rest of us?" people mutter. "There must be something in it for him. The contests are rigged somehow. I notice the president's sister got a big prize."

There is an adage: "Never explain. Your friends don't need it, and your enemies won't believe you." This may be true, but better advice might be: "Never get into a spot where explanations seem necessary." Valuable prizes in a volunteer group do call for explaining, yet no explanations will satisfy outsiders.

There's another danger, too, in dangling pecuniary lures before unpaid workers: the danger of bringing selfish motives into the picture. Your volunteers may stay steadfastly pure in heart, but what will people say about them? "Those guys are in it for what they can get."

And among your volunteers themselves, aren't there a few who might be tempted to cheat just a little? Or whose judgment might be swayed in a fierce fight for loot? Without cheating at all, somebody could forget about helping the organization in his zeal to win the contest. (This was a major headache in the early days of the Little League, for example.) And afterward, mightn't a few angry losers yell Foul?

An inexpensive trophy, a ribbon or pennant, even a battered hat to be worn by a winner when the contestants forgather—any of these can arouse volunteers to prodigious effort. It has been proved often. Hundreds of men run the Boston Marathon every April for a small bronze medal. Many highly talented people are overcome by emotion if given a statuette called an Oscar.

If you're running a contest among volunteers, you'll probably find that the optimum strategy is to offer awards to teams, not individuals. Teamwork is vital in community service. So you need a scheme which stimulates people to pull together. A steak dinner for the winning team, while losers sit on the floor and eat beans, is a typically successful gimmick.

Fight shy of any contest which can start individual rivalries, or jealousy of the champ by the also-rans, suspicion that somebody is a glory-grabber, or worst of all sabotage to prevent somebody from winning. As we saw earlier, recognition is pay. To give one worker more "pay" than his peers is sowing discord. If you must have individual prizes, offer many small ones rather than a few big ones.

Team contests usually are jealousy-proof. A contestant feels a lively glow in belonging to a top team, but he stays anonymous enough to be free of self-seeking.

Above all, the contest must be a pathway to your main purpose, not an end in itself. If you aim to gain new members, raise more money, or increase the number of good swimmers in the town, hold that goal firmly before everyone's eyes. For example, discourage contestants from certifying poor swimmers as good ones just to win the contest. Stay away from big-prize, high-pressure imbroglios. You can inject plenty of color and dash, yet still keep everyone aware that, win or lose, they're helping achieve the main purpose of the campaign.

Spurs in a score card

Another way to nudge unpaid manpower into greater effort is to make sure that everybody knows how everybody else is doing.

Circulating a simple "box score" at short intervals during a project will energize nearly everyone whose name appears on it.

The chairman of one neighborhood financial drive got remarkable results by sending out weekly letters such as this:

From: Charles B. Buckley—Captain, Sustaining
               Membership Team

To: Elwood Gill   Copies to: Maurie Dahlem
     Bob Goldsmith   Keith Monroe
     Bill Henley   Chas. J. Picco
     Harry Stone   Remy Hudson
     Carl Walker

Following is the status of our drive as of January 23:

	Left to Contact	Contacted	Moved, Refused, etc.	Pledged	Amount
Buckley	0	11	1	10	$ 100
Gill	3	10	3	7	65
Goldsmith	10	4	—	4	40
Henley	10	3	—	3	30
Stone	6	8	2	6	50
Walker	9	2	0	2	20
TOTAL	38	38	6	32	$ 305

I will report the above tonight at the District Meeting. Last year our team exceeded its quota by 20%. While our quota is higher this year, we want to beat it by 20% again. So —

Quota	$ 500
Plus 20%	100
Goal	600
To date	305
STILL NEEDED	$ 295

LET'S GET IT DONE — and if possible by Tuesday, January 31.

Call me if I can help!

Charles B. Buckley

CHAPTER 5

When Men Won't Work

If your friend fails you

"I'D LIKE to start a Down with Uplift movement," a store owner said reecntly. "I'm sick of civic work. In business you tell people what to do, and they do it. In these amateur movements, they don't."

His plaint was a common one. Many unpaid workers don't work. But the fault usually lies with their leader as much as with them. A chairman or president must recruit wisely and manage wisely, as we saw in Chapters 3 and 4.

Still, the deepest wisdom in choosing and using men can't always assure a smooth-running team. Sooner or later, if you head any volunteer group, you'll find a few misfits in your entourage: men who do nothing or do the wrong things, such as flouting policy or quarreling with associates. If you can't straighten them out, what can you do about them?

In business you might arbitrarily move them. In communal projects it isn't so easy. Forcing men out can start feuds which cripple a volunteer organization. You need smoother methods.

Of course if it comes to a showdown you *can* remove them. There must be no doubt of this. When you sit in the chairman's hot seat you should have the right, ultimately, to banish any subordinate who can't work with you.

Obviously this doesn't mean that if you organize a staff of ushers in a church, and pick a man who proves unreliable, you can expel him from the church. It does mean that you can quietly drop him from the ushering staff as a last resort.

In Chapter 3 you were advised, "Recruit your subordinates from among your friends." If you followed this advice, perhaps you now feel your plight is the worse for it: you must extract not only a thorn but a friend. How can you ease him out of your committee without offending him?

It's a prickly problem. Yet similar situations come up in business. You've surely encountered the need of diplomatically breaking off a business relationhip. How do you do it?

Presumably your approach is frank and direct. The man you must drop is usually able to see that he hasn't given satisfaction. Therefore you needn't pretend he has. You take the line that his difficulties are due to conditions beyond his control: perhaps an error by you in expecting service that he wasn't in position to give. The impression you convey, if you want to keep his friendship, is that there is very little wrong with him, but a great deal wrong with the burdens placed on him; that a change will be to his advantage.

Very likely you encourage him to do most of the talking. As he talks about his difficulties, about why he hasn't played his appointed role, he comes to see that the easy solution is for him to remove himself. It will be better for everyone. So he does it in gladness and relief, feeling that you are his friend for letting him do so.

Why not follow this process in getting rid of a committee member? The process is easier in volunteer work than in business, for here it isn't embittered by any pain of financial loss.

If you are forthright by nature you may skip all this talk, and summarily oust a committee member by telegram or memo, just as some bosses do in business. But this is a mistake. You incur the lasting enmity not only of the committeeman but of his friends. And remember Ben Franklin's remark, "There are no small enemies." This applies especially to any organization which depends on good will in the community.

As we'll see in the next two sections, there are at least ten ways to get rid of an undesirable committeeman without firing him. Of all these, however, the one already suggested—a tactful but direct talk with the man about his nonperformance—will usually serve you best.

Four ways to decapitate deadheads

The inactive member is the bane of every committee and board. His disaffection dampens the spirit of other members, and irks them because they must carry his share of the load.

Something should be done about him. As chairman, you should do it. You have four alternatives:

1. Let him die on the vine.
2. Detour around him.
3. Arrange his automatic self-removal.
4. Tactfully persuade him to quit (as described in the preceding section).

The first alternative is most often chosen—though it is seldom the best. At least it avoids an open clash. The man lazes through his term, and eventually fades out of everyone's thoughts.

There are times when this is the only discreet way to handle the problem. For example, one church appointed a vigorous junior executive of a corporation as chairman of the vestry's finance committee. To his dismay, it also asked his company president to serve on the committee. The church thought it was strengthening the committee, but it wedged the young chairman into an awkward corner. The older man was formidably intolerant of criticism, and seriously confident that by lending his name to the committee he had done enough.

The young man prudently did not force the issue. He merely asked for an additional man on the committee and let his corporate overlord alone. It is hard to see what else he could have done.

The case illustrates a reason for two principles laid down earlier in this book: a chairman should be free to choose his own committee, and should choose either his own friends or younger men in whom he has confidence.

The "detour" technique sometimes is best with an idler who comes to meetings regularly but does nothing else. One chairman, assigned to prepare publicity material for a Heart Fund drive, had on his committee a powerful newspaper figure he shrank from antagonizing. This man attended committee meetings but never carried out assignments. Still, the chairman could scarcely skip him while giving work to everyone else in the room.

The chairman solved the problem by parceling out all the work to two-man teams. He paired the inactive man with a heavy-duty one who was told in advance that he probably would get no help from his partner. The work was done. The sluggard sat beaming as "his team" reported impressive output. Of course he was not reappointed the following year, but he and the chairman are still friends.

Here is a case where the third stratagem was used: After a few meetings of a citizens' committee for slum clearance, it became plain that several members were chronic absentees. The others therefore contrived a mechanism for their automatic removal.

A pleasant letter went to all members, explaining that they were entering a phase where complete cooperation would be required; therefore any member who missed two successive meetings, or who had to report his inability to carry out an assignment, would be assumed to have resigned and would be replaced. The letter emphasized that members might understandably be too busy, or in poor health, or unable to serve for other compelling reasons. No criticism would be implied in the termination of their membership. It was simply that the committee's work called for people who had time for it.

Each of these three methods has its uses. But each can lead to misunderstandings and grudges. We come back to the method described in the previous section—a clean break by mutual agreement, after friendly discussion—as the best in most cases.

Remember that the truant committeeman knows in his heart that he failed you. Human nature being what it is, he makes excuses to himself. Perhaps he rationalizes that you gave him nothing specific to do—which might be true. Perhaps he has sulked because of some minor irritation which you could easily have dispelled, had you known. Perhaps he thinks, and says to others, that you are impossible to work with.

His attitude may be unfair to the point of insanity, but many otherwise sane men blame someone else when they are at fault. Therefore you will be safer to seek out your inactive subordinate if you can, learn his point of view, and face the issue frankly and affably.

Six ways to stop a troublemaker

Now consider a more explosive situation. Assume that a member of your team is worse than inactive: he is incompatible.

Perhaps he is a well-meaning muddler, who glories in working with you, is tireless and devoted—but botches everything he touches. Even in conversation he is a nuisance, because he talks lengthily without saying much.

Or perhaps he is a fanatic. He is enormously zealous for the cause. He calls down hellfire and brimstone on anyone who shows less zeal. Hackles rise wherever he goes.

Or he may be a rebel. Furiously active in the organization, he derides some of its policies. He plunges into ventures which the organization deems unwise or downright harmful.

Such people moved one president to remark that he never committed murder but read certain obituaries with great satisfaction. The time to exterminate pests is, of course, before they join. They illustrate again why recruiting should be done by intelligent people who personally know the recruits. However, assuming that the mistake has been made, you must move decisively to mend matters.

The good-hearted ineffectual fool may become an asset if you find a safe spot for him. There must be something he can do well. Try to see what it is. Usually nobody tries, and he is passed from committee to committee with no purpose but to move him. This wastes time for everyone concerned. If the man is on your committee, or on your staff, analyze him and give him work at which he will shine. If you cannot do this you should remove him altogether, as resolutely but tactfully as you would the stormy petrels.

How to oust a blatant troublemaker depends on how far he has gone. If you decide to get rid of him soon after he joins, you can sometimes do it gracefully enough to avoid friction. Perhaps the regular day for committee meetings can be set for a time when he cannot attend; then you may explain apologetically that you must substitute someone else who is free to attend meetings.

Perhaps his appointment was for a fixed term, short enough so you are willing to suffer him until it expires. In that case he can be thanked for his service at the end of the term, and not reappointed. This may be a delicate operation if he expects to continue serving, but you can explain casually, "They like us to pass these assignments around."

If neither of the above expedients is suitable, you can overload him with work. Write him or phone him every few days with some new request for help. Keep him so bogged down in unimportant matters that he gets no chance to interfere in important ones. Soon he may silently fade away. If not, pile still heavier and more trivial assignments on to him. His failure to keep up will eventually embarrass him into quitting, or will open the way for you to explain that someone with more free time must replace him.

If he is stirring up such hideous trouble that you dare not use slow methods, you may be able to evoke a thunderbolt from on high. Get some remote superior to insist on his removal. Usually an official at national or regional headquarters of the organization, or perhaps a board of directors, will be willing to issue expulsion orders if his misdeeds are serious. Then you can show him privately that higher-ups have forced your hand; you have no choice but to ask him to withdraw. This of course is not quite candid, but it may save you from losing a friend.

Few of us are ever happy to use such devious tricks. Still, they can sometimes be justified on the ground that they spare a trouble-maker the affront of direct dismissal. Even if you cared nothing for his feelings, openly dropping him would bring on unpleasant scenes almost sure to weaken the committee. Some committee members would draw away, out of distaste for strife. Some outsiders would wonder what the hubbub was about, and whether you and your supporters were right or wrong. The aggrieved man and his friends would probably spread talk against you. Thus there seems ample reason to use roundabout methods on obnoxious adherents.

In most cases, however, the quarrelsome member rouses such antagonism that you need only set him up for the knockout, if no graceful departure can be arranged quickly enough.

When you see the fight approaching, force it to a showdown instead of smoothing it over. Never fall into the old foolishness of cutting off the dog's tail an inch at a time.

Encourage the rest of the committee to speak up against whatever violent pronouncement he has made. Encourage him, if necessary, to reaffirm his stand so fiercely that no compromise is possible. "Either I get my way, or I quit," is what he should say in effect. Thereupon the committee can make the obvious answer, and he walks out.

He is angry, to be sure, but he has left by his own choice. He cannot say he was ousted without a hearing. He can scarcely blame you or any other single person. Even if you do lose his friendship this may be a lesser evil than letting him stay on the committee.

Whatever way you handle him, it is part of your job and within your authority. Unless the group is an elective one (a contingency to be considered in the next section) you have the right to maintain its personnel by both recruiting and removing. Any other arrangement means responsibility without authority, an intolerable combination.

Yet when this is said and done, the fact remains that your removal of a member is a confession that you failed to use him well. You didn't bring out the best in him. Perhaps—unhappy thought —he brought out the worst in you.

There's something about committee work that sets an original thinker against his fellows. They tend to regard him as a heretic. William H. Whyte points out in *The Organization Man:* "Something really bold and imaginative is by its nature divisive, and the bigger the committee, the more people are likely to be offended."

Therefore, before you expunge a nonconformist, perhaps you might consider whether your emotions are too much involved. Are you annoyed at the man because he questions your beliefs or keeps bringing up unpleasant facts you prefer to ignore? May it be healthy for your committee to have a critic in its midst?

Administration is a set of techniques for getting results. When you don't get results, to that extent you fail as an administrator. This may not mean you are at fault. On the other hand, it may. You'll want to look closely to see which is the case.

A president of a large volunteer organization has been widely quoted that "The time to fire a man is the first time you think of it." This trigger-happy outlook can decimate any organization— unless its trigger-men automatically think first of techniques for motivating a worker, analyzing his talents, and adjusting his grievances before a thought of firing ever crosses their minds.

Tactics with your hands tied

We come now to the problem which faces the head of an elected group when he finds inactive or obnoxious members in his group.

Presidents (and paid executives) of school boards, town councils, and some other part-time groups grapple often with this problem. The laziness, bungling, belligerence and policy-bucking described earlier in this chapter seem always to appear in elective bodies.

Here, however, the steersman has less power to quell them. Tactics which were recommended most highly in the foregoing sections can't now be used at all. The moves described less enthusiastically may be the only ones available.

Before we review these tactics in the light of the changed position, let us recognize that leading an elected group doesn't make you its boss. Perhaps part of your job is to suffer fools and enemies.

Even assuming that your clear duty is to oust someone for the good of the organization, you have no authority to do so if the organization has elected him. Moreover, if you do manage to get rid of him, then you weaken your board and your institution. The institution is governed by an elective board for the primary purpose of preventing any one man from governing it—even you.

Differences of opinion are healthy in a board. "Discussed and interrogated administration is the only pure and efficient administration," Woodrow Wilson wrote.

Let us agree, then, that we are not considering means to undermine those who oppose you or who ask annoying questions. We are considering what to do about board members who undeniably handicap and hamstring the movement—either through absenteeism or gross incompetence.

Such incubi are more numerous in elected bodies than in appointed ones. The appointed committeeman was more likely to be efficient because he was selected by a chairman who knew him. The elected man is there, too often, because he took the office for glory or because his constituency could find nobody else who would take it.

This is not to say that the majority of elected board members are unworthy. Most of them are high-powered and high-principled. But the unworthy ones are more of a nuisance, because the chairman does not have the leverage of personal influence to reform or remove them.

When a member of your board shirks, he is not breaking any commitment to you. He owes you nothing. Sometimes you can just disregard him. His absence may cause the board no trouble; obviously you'll assign him no important duties.

Yet it is an unhappy position for you as chairman. You can see, if he can't, how much the organization loses by his nonfeasance. To make matters worse, he may easily be re-elected to term after term.

The only way to eliminate him short of mayhem is by vote of the group which elected him. You can't prudently suggest this to his group. He'll hear of it and resent it, as will his supporters.

Your remedy lies if anywhere in making sure that his constituency lacks, and knows it lacks, the benefits of being actively represented. Decisions it would dislike are made at meetings because its elected spokesman is silent. Reservations for desirable tables at annual meetings, for the best periods at camp, for preferred places in the organization's doings of whatever kind—these should go to groups represented at your meetings, on the assumption that those unrepresented are uninterested. Setbacks of this kind may jolt a group into electing a conscientious representative.

The eager idiot whose only fault is lack of intelligence gives you even more trouble. He is ever-present at meetings, and he offers himself headlong for every assignment. When his term is up he is almost sure to be re-elected. Therefore you will have to learn to live with him.

If anyone is available who can appraise his talents and put them to use, this is your salvation. Otherwise, all you can do is make sure he is given joint assignments shared by competent men, who understand that he is erratic, and who will leap to undo whatever harm he does.

The truculent cranks are most irksome of all. The fact that they are cantankerous should never obscure the possibility that they may be right. Dissidents are not always diplomatic, but they probably are elected because they represent the views of a number of people.

As suggested earlier, a downright wrecker can sometimes be nullified by loading him with work, by persuading higher authorities to oust him for dangerous subversion, or by presenting such a phalanx of opposition that he resigns in a huff. Give the matter long consideration before you attempt such maneuvers, however. Just because he infuriates you is no sign that he endangers your organization.

CHAPTER 6

You're on a Committee

*Our part in the group can no longer be a
passive one: it is not enough to belong; one
must act and lead; and our achievement of
balance will be meaningless unless it makes
us ready, on demand, to take our turn at
any or all the roles in a group; to command
and to think, to emotionalize and energize,
to assimilate and obey.*

—LEWIS MUMFORD

DID the last three chapters give the impression that the chairman
is the one important member of a committee? We hope not. It
isn't so.

We also hope you won't ignore some sections of this book because they seem to be addressed to chairmen or presidents, while
you are neither. The whole book is slanted for you, the man in
the club, on the committee, on the board. Advice to a chairman
is talk to you over his shoulder. It hints and pleads that you won't
be any of the various kinds of "problem member" who raise a
chairman's pulse. If you know the job of the man at the head of
the table you can do your own job better, just as a football player
is more effective if he knows what his teammates are up to.

We especially hope that committeemen won't skip Chapter 7.

They need to understand what the chairman is trying to do, and why.

What to do when you join

Like a parachutist dropped in a strange desert, your first job as a new committeeman is to get your bearings. This may entail some preliminary homework. Possibly you should look into the history of the committee—why it was formed, what it has done—by browsing in the minutes or chatting with an old-timer. Then you'll need to know the committee's future aims, and its place in the larger organization. The handbook or bylaws may clarify this.

Less obviously, but still usefully, you might inquire about the background of your fellow committeemen. Why were these kinds of people chosen? What is their common denominator?

Your homework may not give you enough answers. Then further probing is indicated, either at your first few meetings or outside. A University of Michigan study of group work crystallized certain responsibilities which members of any group should shoulder. Heading the list was: *If objectives are vague, insist they be made clear.*

This may sound obvious or superfluous to you. A committee with vague objectives? Improbable. Committeemen who don't know why they're there? Impossible. But a newcomer often finds more fog than he expects. The casework committee of a social agency may meet for months and listen to synopses of cases without anyone asking, "What is this committee supposed to do about them, if anything?" Boy Scout officials often meet men who say proudly, "Oh yes, I'm in Scouting. On the troop committee, I think. I don't know just why they have it, but you fellows seem to think it's necessary." This in spite of the detailed description of the job of the troop committee on papers which the committeeman has signed.

You may find your committee's broad objective spelled out in the bylaws and still not know what specific targets are now on the horizon. Almost every lodge and service club has a boys' work committee, for example, with duties delineated in literature from its national office; but the literature can't tell precisely what your committee's projects are for this year.

So ask questions. Press for clear answers. Is your group supposed to be judging, investigating, advising, planning, or creating? Your questions may stir up thought, which is unsettling but healthy.

Once you know the committee's role, make sure of your personal role within it. A committee to buy a gift for your departing pastor won't present any enigma, but a standing committee usually is set up with a division of duties—sometimes formal, sometimes only tacit.

Each member is (or should be) given that slice of the work which interests him most, or which he can do best. But he isn't always told, unless he asks, what the committee thinks he can do. Whatever it is in your case—potent connections, or a sharp pencil at figuring costs, or a shrewd eye for legal pitfalls—the sooner you know, the better.

This preliminary reconnoitering serves other purposes beyond orienting you. You and the chairman get better acquainted while you're quizzing him. Also, your interest and enthusiasm are likely to rise; you'll go into your first meeting already warmed up.

Your first meeting

If you're a newcomer, the old-timers will be sizing you up. You won't want to seem too shy or too brash. And if the whole committee is new, the problem is multiplied. Of course the chairman's job includes melting these invisible barriers, but he needs help.

Eugene Peckham's *Dynahelps for Democratic Leaders* gives

suggestions about conferences in industry which apply here. He stresses the need for quickly fusing "just a gathering of people" into a team. He advises a new committeeman to get this process started by what he calls a systematic warm-up.

His first suggestion is "Come early." Locate the meeting place. Familiarize yourself with its facilities.

Then chat with every member, if you can, before the meeting is called to order. Such chatting gives you a chance to mention who you are and why you're interested, and to evoke similar information from the others. If you do this casually, with a smile, you'll no longer be a stranger by the time the meeting starts. "Establish as many two-group relationships as you can," Peckham advises, "and help others do likewise."

Say something!

"Silence is the virtue of fools," according to Francis Bacon. It certainly isn't golden in a committee meeting. A silent committeeman may learn a lot, but he contributes nothing, and may dampen the spirit of his cohorts.

Silence worries people. A periodic brief comment reassures them, even if it's only a banal word or two. But you can contribute more. Why not ask a question occasionally? Don't worry about sounding naïve. The others know you're new. They'll welcome your questions as a sign of interest. Besides, your fresh approach may light up something they overlooked.

Before long you can start expressing opinions. Not lengthily, of course, nor bluntly, but helpfully. Unless someone else has adequately stated the same opinion, say what you think about every issue that comes up. Perhaps you can do it as Ben Franklin did:

> When another asserted something that I thought an error, I denied myself the pleasure of contradicting him abruptly. . . .

I began by observing that in certain circumstances his opinion would be right, but in the present case there *appear'd* or *seem'd* to me some difference.

Or perhaps you can function as Paul L. Johnson does. He is a seasoned committeeman, a mover and shaker in a dozen civic enterprises, as well as a full-time executive of Pacific Telephone Company. At every meeting his pencil is flying over a large pad. He jots down every opinion and suggestion voiced. After a while he synthesizes and points up what the others have said, the areas of agreement and disagreement, and his own judgment in the light of his experience. That's why he's a famous old pro at committee work.

Chairmen often have trouble getting everyone to participate usefully. You can help. If you see that Jones is too shy to speak, you can say, "I'd like to hear what Mr. Jones thinks about this." If the conversation strays off the subject you can herd it back. If someone has a good point but isn't getting through to the others, you can tactfully rephrase it so they grasp it.

When you see that another member doesn't understand the committee's aims, you ought to tip off the chairman on the side, so he can either enlighten the erring member or ask you to do so.

Another, more subtle, help you can give is simply to show enthusiasm. Let everyone see that you're interested and loyal.

Don't make these mistakes

There are as many ways to be obnoxious in committee as there are in a card party. They include heckling, second-guessing, monologuing, dogmatizing, pontificating, belittling, and quarreling.

Rather than list them all, let's bundle them up and dismiss them in one British phrase: Don't be beastly. No committeeman tries to be but many are, without half trying. To avoid it keep a hard eye on yourself, a tight rein on your ego, and an open mind toward others.

Another whole constellation of errors—genial ones—might be catalogued under the general heading of Distractions. Telling a long involved story; starting a debate on a side issue; joking with a neighbor while an earnest colleague is speaking. Watch yourself, and don't take offense if someone says, "We aren't getting very far with the business of the meeting." Committee meetings are faster and more fruitful when everyone sticks to the subject and saves funny stories for the coffee-klatsch afterward.

A third type of mistake is overhelpfulness. Remember that many chairmen are inexperienced, uneasy, and self-conscious. A helpful remark which implies criticism may throw them into a tizzy. If you think your chairman needs advice, you can almost always be more helpful by advising him in private and with tact. You may happen to know that some members disagree with his views but won't say so; or that they're losing heart; or that a pet theory of his is wrong. You may have brilliant ideas to make meetings less boring or more productive. But your bombshells will all be better received when you're alone with the chairman. If you broach them in open meeting he may be upset not only at the implied rebuke but at interference with his program. He can give them more judicious thought if he hears them in a quiet corner. And if he turns down your proffered help you won't have been publicly squelched.

Another error is inviting somebody to join the committee—or, more commonly, asking the committee to invite him—without first consulting the chairman alone. He knows what kind of people he wants. There may be reasons, which he can't state openly, for not wanting your candidate.

All the above blunders are fairly common, easy to make, but

easy to avoid when you understand protocol. One other mistake, however, is ubiquitous and persistent: talking too much.

It's hard for a talker to know how much is too much. Enthusiasm and good ideas are assets to a committee. Good or not, ideas are welcome to any chairman who understands the democratic process. But many a man becomes as gabby as a circus barker without ever realizing it. Logorrhea, like halitosis, is a fault which friends are loth to mention. How can one detect it in oneself?

If you notice people fidgeting or staring into space when you talk, you talk too much. If a chairman politely cuts in—"We appreciate the contributions you've made, but I suggest you hold your other points until later," or if you are several times asked to speak *briefly*, it may dawn on you. A major offender will sooner or later be chided by the chairman or someone else, or quietly dropped. But even when you're aware of your bad habit, it's hard to correct.

Peckham, in his *Dynahelps* mentioned previously, offers prescriptions to people who realize they talk too much and want to cut down. One is to put their thought in writing before they speak. This makes them clarify and condense, and gives other people more time to be heard.

Another is to ask a question rather than launch into a statement. The question can be framed to draw the statement out of someone else, usually in shorter form.

A third is simply to lower the voice. "The chances are you have a strident voice," Peckham says, "or you wouldn't so successfully overwhelm others who want to talk. Turn down your volume."

The garrulous are chronic interrupters. "Practice yielding," Peckham says. "When someone tries to interrupt you, let him. When a silence falls, wait for someone else to break it."

If you can do that, you've kicked the habit.

If you're in the minority

Harmony is sweet. It's almost indispensable to teamwork. But harmony is a matter of atmosphere. It means friendliness rather than hostility. It doesn't mean that members always agree.

"No government can be long secure without a formidable opposition," Disraeli said. His paradox is a keystone of community enterprise. A mature group can differ yet remain friends.

In fact, a good working rule is that majorities are usually wrong at first. New ideas stick in the craw. Old ideas seem sacred. Emotions and personalities trample logic. Vital facts are often invisible (no committee ever has *all* the facts).

Therefore it's a duty of a good committee member to question everything silently, and to speak out when answers continue to elude him. Why is this being done? Why this way? Are there better ways? Are pertinent facts ignored?

Most of us shrink a little from asking such questions. We know our colleagues prefer to feel that everyone agrees with them. As Ordway Tead points out, even in the midst of disagreeing most of us abhor disagreement. Stendhal wrote, "The approval of others is a certificate of resemblance." For the sake of peace, and the approval of others, we tend to keep quiet. But in our stronger moments we remember Abraham Lincoln's stern reminder, "To sin by silence when they should protest makes cowards out of men."

Your protest can be couched as mild questions, thus ruffling fewer feathers. A question can be a welcome stimulant to a fair-minded committee. Figuring out the answer may lead people to change their view. On the other hand, their answer may explain their view so you yourself agree with it.

But sometimes your quizzing will leave you still in disagreement. What then?

First, of course, you need to re-examine your own thinking.

APATID ☐

PZ ☐☐☐

:ARD

☐ ☐ ☐☐☐☐☐☐☐☐☐☐☐☐☐☐☐
   MI   Last

☐☐☐☐☐☐☐☐☐☐☐☐☐☐☐☐☐
Route Number

☐☐☐☐☐☐☐☐☐☐☐☐☐☐☐☐

☐☐☐☐☐☐☐☐☐☐☐☐☐☐☐☐

☐☐☐☐☐☐-☐☐☐☐

☐☐☐

☐☐☐

•r statistical purposes so we can serve y•

NCE

define in
Spanish

1. Funcution.

2 goal.

3. eforts

4. Fiesta
   Coerdanater

5. empresa
   english.

How does it look from the other side? Are you sure of your facts? Is your opposition based on a pet theory, or a pet peeve? Our own rationalizing has a way of sounding very rational to ourselves. Try to think it out, and perhaps talk it out with some frank friend, before you plant yourself firmly in a minority stance.

Having done all this, don't back down because the majority is unmoved. If the good of your group demands that the others change their opinion, it's up to you to persuade them. How you'll do it depends on the situation. There are times to fight, times to explain, times to conciliate. Usually you should be diplomatic, sometimes you should be silent, occasionally you must be fiery.

A man we'll call Sterling Buck joined an organization something like the Phobia Foundation. He found it composed almost entirely of parents of children suffering from the disease which the agency was formed to combat. To these parents he seemed cold and ignorant, because he hadn't been through what they had. But Mr. Buck realized that these devoted souls didn't have much influence with people of power and property—which was what they needed to finance a health agency. Nor did they know how to stay on good terms with doctors and hospitals. Before much could be accomplished they'd have to give up control of the foundation and put it in the hands of a board with prestige, diplomacy and connections.

He couldn't tell them so, of course. They'd simply force him out. But Mr. Buck wanted the Phobia Foundation to succeed. So he sat quietly at meetings. On the outside he worked to interest certain wealthy men; and in time he got them to subscribe an adequate fund, with the proviso that they control the spending of it. Slowly this group evolved into a board of directors, while the larger group of dedicated parents became an advisory council.

Sometimes the majority is merely apathetic. The boys' work committee of a service club was plodding comfortably along, taking a few orphans to ball games and giving them a Christmas party. But one member, John Brown, got excited about the work of a youth center in the worst part of town. It faced bankruptcy. He urged his committee to dash to the rescue. But the other committeemen thought this too much trouble for a small group of boys.

It was John Brown's fiery table-thumping enthusiasm which finally broke them down. He told them stories of boys the center was helping. He reminded them that these boys' parents would never support such an enterprise. "That's why it's a blighted area," he barked. "These kids will rot in the alleys if we let the center close." He advocated a bigger, stronger center which the service club could promote. To clinch it, he had figures at his finger tips. He proved that all this could be done with the committee's available budget. He swept everyone along with him, and the club eventually took deep pride in the project. But if Brown had been quiet and patient, the youth center would have died.

In Chaos Falls, New York, one man kicked up a storm over the basketball team of the Young Pirates Association. The team was headed for the championship of an intercity Pirate league when this skeptical program committeeman asked himself why. He pried. He discovered that the team wasn't drawn from regular Young Pirate membership at all. The coach had combed the city for stars, and signed them as nominal members of the YPA. He drilled them daily, forsaking all others.

The skeptic was smart enough not to get angry, although the rabid boosters of the team were angry at him. He quietly showed them the facts. No genuine Young Pirates were playing. The team of ringers monopolized the gym floor and the coach's time, which should have been used for the benefit of boys who really needed it. Cool exposition finally turned his minority view into the majority one. The Chaos Falls club withdrew from the league and switched to intramural play for dozens of its own boys.

Sometimes it's better to roll with the punches and conciliate an angry majority rather than fight it. (A Chinese proverb says, *By fighting you never get enough, by yielding you get more than you expected.*) For example, a church board was told, correctly, that a Scout troop sponsored by the church had broken new chairs in the recreation hall, and torn the carpet. The board exploded. It decreed that the troop must meet elsewhere.

Boys will be boys, as their fathers know. Two fathers were on the church board. But they also knew that the elderly majority of the board would not consider boyishness an extenuation for damaged property. So these minority members counseled with the Scoutmaster and his troop committee, and later with the Scouts. All hands were ashamed of the damage wreaked, eager to fix it, and glad to promise that rough games would henceforth be played only outdoors. This news was taken to the church board. In addition, the troop proposed to include service to its sponsor as part of its activities in future, beginning by rebinding the church's old hymnbooks. This ingenious compromise mollified the board, so the troop wasn't banished after all.

But there are also times when a conscientious committeeman can't duck a fight. In San Diablo, California, a new member of the building committee of the Knights of the Cauliflower found that the committee was quietly preparing to fire the janitor. Why? Well, he was uppity. Then too, one of the members had an uncle who wanted the job. The new committeeman found that the present janitor was working like a beaver, and had been for two years. Nobody could point to any flaw in his work. It was just that the committeemen disliked him. Their new committee member couldn't convert them. So he wrote a letter of resignation, explaining that he refused to be a party to unjust dismissal of a good janitor. He sent copies to all officers of the lodge. In the ensuing hubbub the building committee was discharged, and the janitor kept his job.

Of course a minority member isn't always right, although the human brain is so constructed that he usually thinks he is. And even when he is, sometimes surrender is smart. Being a loyal loser isn't always cowardly. It may be better to let a group make a mistake than to try to stop it.

For example, a YMCA leader planned a camping trip to a lake where canoes were available. But an unsupervised canoeist had drowned there in the recent past. So the camp committee was dead set against any canoeing for its boys. The leader was saddened, because he was an expert aquatics man and a strict enforcer of safety rules. He might have forced the committee to let him use canoes by threatening not to go unless they did.

But he applied a lesson of history pointed out by Liddell Hart in his book *Strategy:* "The most satisfactory peace settlements, even for the stronger side, proved to be those made by negotiation rather than by a decisive military issue." The camp leader knew that imposing his will on the camp committee might make them so angry that they wouldn't work with him in future. He dropped the issue. The canoes weren't worth a major battle. A year later the committee let him use them.

A PTA committee, working to raise money for a school cafeteria, rejected a local merchant's offer of a new gas range because he was running for the legislature, and many PTA people were backing his opponent. They thought his offer was a bid to woo voters. One committeeman was convinced that the gift would have no impact on the political race, and that the PTA should accept because it needed the gas range. But he shrugged and said nothing. He knew that to stand up for his belief would make the PTA a political battlefield. Teamwork in the committee was worth more than the gift.

Before you force an issue, ask yourself: Is a principle at stake?

H. A. Overstreet's *The Mature Mind* points out the significance of this question:

On a tablet in front of the Old South Meeting House, in Boston, are words that describe our Revolutionary forefathers as "worthy to raise issues." They knew which things were important and which were unimportant. A person has to be mature to be worthy to raise issues. Most of the small frictions in life that destroy mutual confidence and enjoyment come from raising issues that are not worth raising—and most of the social inertias and timidities that keep our world from moving toward its ideals express a reluctance to raise issues that should be raised.

CHAPTER *7*

You're the Chairman

Greatness does not depend on the size of your command, but on the way you exercise it.

—MARSHAL FERDINAND FOCH

Lost in the fog?

So YOU'RE a chairman. Chairman of what? Of a working committee, or a board? Let's get the distinction clear.

Webster defines a committee as "a group of persons chosen to act in some capacity." A board, he says, is "a group of administrators." This basic difference isn't always plain in everyday usage. There are three types of groups often called committees, but only two meet the dictionary definition. Here are the three:

1) A committee formed to do a single, specific, short-term job —pick a campsite, perhaps, or nominate a slate of officers, or organize a charity show. In military terminology, it might be called a task force. In socialese, it is often referred to as an *ad hoc* committee, or a working committee.

2) A standing committee. Over a long term it deals with all matters which fall in one broad category. It might be the membership committee, or ways and means committee, or publicity committee.

3) A committee—really a board, though it isn't always called so—which supervises the work of other people. These people may be the paid experts in the Heart Fund office, or the church pastor and his assistants, or the caseworkers in a social agency. They may be unpaid technicians such as a Scoutmaster and his staff (supervised by the troop committee) or a corps of Red Cross volunteer swim instructors (supervised by the chapter's water-safety committee). Such committees usually set policy and administer it. They don't ordinarily tackle detailed on-the-spot jobs such as working committees and standing committees do. If you head this type of committee-board, you'll find additional advice in Chapter 10.

Whichever kind you head, your first duty as chairman is to take aim. What is your committee expected to accomplish? What is its reason for being?

Two million people in the United States are serving on committees for social betterment. Many of these committees are constantly collapsing and re-forming, with ever-changing membership; their members feel they aren't accomplishing much. Why? Primarily because their objectives are too vague.

A committee should have a clear purpose—not necessarily a quota to meet or a building to construct, but some plainly defined function to perform. This may be to study and solve a stated problem, or to grapple with specific kinds of situation if and when they arise.

Whatever it is, it should be understood by all members, including those who join late. You, as chairman, have the responsibility for this. It is vitally important. Defining your objectives is usually easy with a working committee, hard with a standing committee, harder yet with an administrative committee.

Too many meetings?

Members of volunteer committees often complain that "we have too many meetings." If your cohorts say this about your committee, what they really mean is that not enough happens at your meetings.

A meeting isn't distasteful per se. Poker games and golf foursomes are meetings, but the participants don't complain of the frequency. Sessions of any committee can be richly satisfying. If members are well chosen they enjoy each other. They come out of a desire to help. When they feel they actually are being helpful, they'll be enthusiastic. They droop only when hours pass in rambling unproductive talk.

Accomplishment is the key. Better no meeting than one without a plan to accomplish something. A committee should move measurably closer to its objectives at each meeting.

This is easy for a committee with physical work to do, such as analyzing lists of prospective donors, or revising a brochure. If you are chairman you need to be a good stage manager. Set your stage ahead of time. Don't be caught at the last minute hunting a janitor to unlock a door, or dragging too many chairs into a too-small room, or trying to be heard against a basketball game across the hall. Make your committee comfortable. Is there parking space nearby? Is the room properly heated and ventilated? If your committee has writing to do, provide a big table; don't expect people to sit on sofas and write on their knees. Distribute pencils and note paper. Provide ash trays. Maybe a blackboard will be helpful. Get all your working materials ready in advance.

But when a committee's function is to make plans and decisions, then the chairman's job is harder. In fact, some say it is impossible. Ralph Cordiner of General Electric says, "G.E. has no place for committees as decision-making bodies. A committee moves at the speed of its least informed member and too often is used as a way of sharing irresponsibility." The *Operations Manual* of the Junior Chamber of Commerce warns that a committee or board "is not a planning agency. It is incapable of any intelligent planning. Plans are better made by individuals than by groups—and never, never by groups so large as the board. Your board is a deliberative, policy-forming body. It confines itself to considering plans and courses of action previously worked out in detail by individuals or small committees. Planning by the board means planning failure."

We revere Mr. Cordiner. We cherish the Jaycees. Yet their axioms may not always apply outside their own organizations. Some civic committees must, and can, plan and decide.

An adroit chairman won't let the least informed member slow everyone down too much, as Mr. Cordiner fears, or let the committee dodge responsibility. He will, as the Jaycee manual wisely advises, get detailed planning done by individuals outside the meeting. But sometimes, before this planning can be parceled out, the committee should discuss the purpose of the plans and the general direction to take.

Such a deliberative meeting calls for groundwork by the chairman. He should let his members know what problems are coming up (see Chapter 8) and try to stir up a sense of urgency. As the French say, "To get an audience, create a disturbance."

Perhaps the chairman should suggest several possible solutions to the problems he has posed, among which the committee can make a choice. Or he might arrange for someone else to propose these solutions at the meeting. He may want to talk ahead of time with members who don't understand an issue and might be hostile. Occasionally the real reason for handling a problem one way instead of another can't be brought out in open meeting, for fear of hurting someone's feelings, perhaps.

But suppose a meeting's sole purpose is to give out information? Such meetings are held to kick off a finance campaign or a membership drive. They may look simple to the chairman. The physical work of making up lists and kits is done in advance. The planning and deciding is over with. Members at the meeting have nothing to do but listen to instructions.

While the chairman may feel fine about this, members may not. With nothing to do, they naturally feel they are doing nothing. They may consider all those elaborate plans bunk. Why waste an evening on palaver which could be put on paper and sent in the mail? Why not just distribute the lists, and let the members start work?

You, as chairman, know that half the people who get written instructions never read them carefully. And you know that your drive, whatever it is, needs enthusiasm. The purpose of convoking your people is to brief them and enthuse them. But this is the meeting where you'll need all your ingenuity to avoid the "too many meetings" plaint. Somehow you must make each member feel he accomplished something and was glad he came.

One way to do this is to build "audience participation" into your program. Give your captive audience something to do. Instead of assigning quotas, you might ask each team to caucus briefly and decide its own quota. You might encourage teams to challenge each other: either in competition to see which meets its self-determined quota sooner, or which brings in the highest actual total. If you do this, don't announce the prizes as your own offering. Instead, let the members wrangle a bit among themselves as to what the prizes shall be, if any, and how they shall be won.

To repeat: Accomplishment is the key. Not accomplishment by the chairman of his purpose, but accomplishment by the members of *their* purpose. And it should happen at every meeting.

Too much talk?

Civic chairmen commonly believe that "committee meetings should be interesting and inspiring." So far so good. But they go off the deep end with a corollary that members will be interested and inspired by listening to reports.

No matter how enchanting the reports, committeemen soon tire of coming to hear them. Of course reports are necessary, and valuable for various reasons. If a member knows he'll be expected to report, he'll want to do something worth reporting. Indeed, if he does a satisfying job, he'll enjoy telling about it. "When some men discharge an obligation," Mark Twain said, "you can hear the report for miles around."

Then too, a chairman needs reports in order to know what's getting done or not getting done. Unhappily, however, a report seldom interests or inspires anybody except the man who makes it and the chairman who receives it. Other members wait restlessly for their own chance to report—or, having reported, plot how to slip away quietly.

So here you have a major problem, Mr. Chairman.

Private reports to you from your committeemen will give you the data you need. Can you make such a solitary interview (or letter) a satisfying thrill to the man? Probably you can, if you thank him perceptively, accurately, and warmly. You might also summarize his report yourself at the meeting. If there are many reports, maybe they can be mimeographed for the members to read. Maybe each man can be recognized with a public word of commendation and some amiable gesture such as a carnation for his buttonhole.

Whatever you do, don't let routine reports clog your agenda. Ideally, a member would announce, "Mission accomplished," whereupon the committee would proceed to discuss, "So what's the next mission?" But if a report reveals difficulties which the committee can help overcome, you'll usually want to have the member repeat his report briefly at the meeting, so the committee can decide what to do. The report which interests members is the one which involves them in making new decisions.

But even decision-making can be dull, if you let the talk get rambling or shallow. Members of the United States Olympic Games Committee once spent a whole afternoon arguing whether team members should wear white or colored pocket handkerchiefs during the opening parade. Beware of too much talk about too little!

Showmanship isn't the answer

In Euphoria, Massachusetts, the camp committee of the Friendly Cannibals met last spring to tackle the job of promoting attendance at summer camp. There were fifteen men on the committee—one from each district subcommittee to recruit campers from that district.

The chairman wanted his meeting to be "interesting and inspiring." So he arranged for a series of handsome young campers to stand up and tell the committee how swell the camp was, how thrilled somebody felt when he passed a swimming test, how excited another was when he caught a snake. There were well-sung camp songs. The meeting ended with the chairman's exhortation to "see to it that every boy has the chance to spend a week at our wonderful camp." It was typical of major committee meetings in many youth organizations.

No doubt some committeemen felt a rosy glow, momentarily. Perhaps they all were glad their camp seemed popular.

On the other hand, many of them may have been sophisticated enough to realize that the winsome kids in the little show were hand-picked and probably coached in lines written by the staff; and that uncoached campers might tell a different story.

At best this committee was entertained and briefly pleased. At worst it may have been bored—and irritated at the waste of an evening. The meeting was staged with showmanship, but it wasn't "a stimulus to creative thought or action," which is the dictionary definition of inspiration.

You certainly must interest your committee. If possible you should inspire it; an emotional lift puts more drive into any group. But you won't interest a busy man for long with vaudeville or cheery reports. To interest him, a meeting must get something done with his help.

Contrast the above meeting with one held, in virtually identical circumstances, by the Young Pirates Association in Angelton, to stir up summer camp enrollment. Its camp committee also consisted of district camping chairmen. But the agenda was planned to keep every man busy throughout the meeting. It went like this:

1. Each district reports on firm reservations already made. Tabulate on blackboard, showing space still available. **10 min.**

2. Award trophy to high man, and collect "fines" from districts more than 25% below commitment. **5 min.**

3. Acceptance by each district of a quota of space still available (reserving 100 spaces for Central Dist.) **20 min.**

4. Agreement on deadline for reservation of quota spaces, after which all space thrown open **10 min.**

5. Challenges **10 min.**

6. Report from Central District on leadership and transportation needs **5 min.**

7. What districts can help with leadership or transport? Get commitments or set deadline dates where member needs time to get commitment **20 min.**

8. Announce bus schedules for committee's inspection visit to camp next Saturday. Leave 1:30 return 9:30

There was very little sit-and-listen time. Each man was thinking hard. He had to declare the camp reservations his district wanted. If he guessed too low, some of his Young Pirate crews might not get space. If he guessed too high, he might be "challenged" by some other committeeman, to whom he would owe cigars or a dinner if his quota wasn't filled. Next he had to help decide how long reservations should be kept open, and commit his district to help bring boys from Central District slums to camp.

When the ninety-minute meeting ended, each district had its camp reservations, and each committeeman had a clear idea of what to do next. He went home full of excitement about camp.

You too can run such a meeting. Just figure out a way to put everyone into the act. Remember that busy committeemen aren't much interested in hearing reports, or in watching a show. To inspire them, simply let them see the significance of the job they can do. To interest them, plan a meeting where they do part of that job.

The fallacy of fixed dates

Some chairmen of working committees cling blindly to a calendar. Even if there's no work on hand, they call a meeting anyway because "we meet on the first Tuesday of every month." They whip up an agenda of generalities and irrelevancies, then wonder why attendance dwindles.

They've mentally transposed their working committee with an administrative committee, which *should* meet regularly to judge and act upon the plans and recommendations of people whom it supervises.

A small committee, geared for a definite project, may meet weekly or even oftener while gaining momentum. Once under way, it should meet only on call. Let's say it is a committee to draw plans for a new church. Shouldn't most of this work be done outside the meetings? One member can dicker for bids or permits. Another can talk with architects. A mass of detail will need untangling by individuals before the group can go further. When the time is ripe a meeting can be called. It will discuss steps taken since the last meeting; approve or change them; consider data gathered by members; divide up assignments for next time.

Of course some work can be done better by a group than by individuals: cooperative manual labor, or nominating a slate of officers, or interviewing prospects for a staff position. But even these must wait until preliminary work is done outside, and all the needed material (raw, paper, or human) has been processed. Why tackle an important job half-prepared, just to meet a fixed meeting date? Better wait until everything is ready, then call your meeting with ample advance notice.

But the opposite rule applies to a supervisory or administrative committee, which is really a board. Boards must meet regularly, so their members can learn what is happening on the firing line and what their front-line personnel plan to do next. Special meetings may be needed too, in emergencies. But the regular meeting assures the working staff of the opportunity to bring up plans for approval and support.

However, a committee chairman should face the fact that fixed-date meetings are harder to make productive and attractive to his committeemen. So prepare carefully!

They call it group dynamics

In the last decade a long shelf of books and monographs about group dynamics has appeared. They expound techniques by which people working together face-to-face (but preferably not toe-to-toe) can get worth-while results. You may want to browse through some of this material in your public library or bookstore.

Some of it points out the dangers of striving too hard for harmony. This is a common weakness of chairmen. In describing some of these peace-loving leaders, Reuel Denny says in *Commentary:*

> They were planning a strategy to prevent the bright and talkative men from intimidating the others; they were going to get participation even if they, in a nice way, had to slug somebody.

Bonaro Overstreet adds in *Understanding Fear:*

> Even where the set-up has been arranged to provide for disagreements . . . there is often a dread lest someone clash too strongly with someone else. One man who has had intensive experience in training leaders for such groups has told me that one of his hardest problems is to find trainees who do not become uneasy in the presence of an honest conflict of ideas.

And William H. Whyte's *The Organization Man* warns us of—

> The hunch that wasn't followed up. The controversial point that didn't get debated. The idea that was suppressed. Were these acts of group cooperation or of individual surrender?

Very well. Let's assume you believe in honest conflict of ideas, so you let opinions clash in your committee. Teeth are bared. Fingers wag. What should you do, at the head of a storm-tossed table?

First, be impartial. Second, be friendly.

Remember that a chairman should keep his own opinions out of sight. Your job is to get all the facts and views before the meeting, as clearly as possible, and then work toward a decision.

The more tempers boil, the calmer you need to be. Do your best to keep the disagreement friendly and impersonal. Use your tact, your smile, your pleasant voice, your sense of humor. Point out areas of agreement. But don't try to smother disagreements. If your members were in full accord before they met, there'd be no point in meeting.

When disagreements are deep-rooted, your tactic is to induce the disputants to listen to each other. Ask each to state the position of the opposition before stating his own. Insist that his version of the opposite view be accepted as accurate before you allow debate to go on.

Keep the group on the subject. "Does the Chair hear a motion?" is a compelling question. Once you hear a motion, rule out all irrelevancies until the group has thrashed out and voted on it. Keep reminding everyone of the issue as stated in the motion. But remember that nobody has power to cut off the discussion of the motion simply by shouting "Question!" A firm grasp of Robert's *Rules of Order* is a great help to a beleaguered chairman.

Now let's consider quite a different predicament in which chairmen often find themselves. Suppose you see that certain work will need to be done by somebody between this meeting and the next. So you call for volunteers. Silence falls. No one volunteers.

What now? You as chairman can either turn to someone and ask him, "Bob, will you take this on?" or you can announce that since there are no volunteers the job will perforce not be done. A third choice, popular in some organizations but harmful in the long run, is to say, "Since John Doolittle is absent I'll appoint him to do this job." Everybody laughs, and somebody says, "That'll teach John to come to meetings and defend himself."

Maybe John will do the job, and maybe he won't. If he does it, he won't be happy about it. Nobody likes to be ordered around. Intsead of appointing him *in absentia*, you'll stand a better chance of getting his wholehearted help if you approach him personally and explain your need for him.

This is what you should have done in the first place, either with Bob or John or whoever is best fitted for the task. Calling for volunteers in open meeting is poor practice. Out of every ten calls for volunteers you'll get one good man, two or three unsuitable men, and no response at all the rest of the time.

Remember that the average person feels uncomfortable about volunteering, unless he is in a group which he knows well. He thinks he'll look conceited or pushy to strangers. He fears he may be pre-empting a job which somebody else would like. And, being average, he has many moments when he'd simply prefer to let George do it. But he might be perfectly willing, even eager, to do the job if you asked him privately in advance.

Your mass meeting

You've been named, we'll suppose, to be chairman of a large public gathering called to discuss a public problem. Perhaps it's a PTA meeting, up in arms about some startling act by the school board or the superintendent. Perhaps it's a convocation of spokesmen from many groups which want something done about the plight of newly arrived Hungarian refugees or Indian tribesmen in the city. Perhaps it's a town meeting to plan for driving rodents out of the woods; John Hersey brilliantly recounts one such turbulent session in his novel *The Marmot Drive*.

Whatever its purpose, a large "action meeting" is hard to handle. Too many people want the floor. Irrelevancies abound. Nonstop orators lurk everywhere. Passions may run high.

Some chairmen of mass meetings try to prepare in advance by writing key questions for discussion on a blackboard, or mimeographing them and handing them to all comers. Such thoughtful preparations are usually futile. The instant the meeting opens, people are on their feet clamoring, "These questions aren't properly worded. . . . These aren't the most important issues anyhow. . . . Why do we sit here talking when action is needed? . . . How can we act when we don't know the facts? . . . I protest . . . I move . . . I suggest . . . I demand . . ."

If you are chairman of such a shindy, your trouble lies in the fact that you're leading a discussion group which is much too big for orderly discussion. Six or eight people can come to agreement. Sixty can't. Nevertheless, mass meetings are part of the American way of meeting crises. So techniques have evolved to help chairmen avoid chaos. Here is a twelve-step plan for running a mass meeting:

1. Open the meeting by explaining the procedure you'll follow. Your voice and manner should be pleasant, but authoritative. Make it clear that everyone will have a chance to be heard, under your ground rules. Your rules should fix a time limit for every speaker.

2. Ask for agreement (by voice vote or show of hands) on your proposed rules. You'll usually get it freely at this stage, but if you wait until later to ask for it, you're in for a long wrangle.

3. Get all the facts out in the open before allowing any proposals for action. This may involve an opening statement by one or more well-informed people. But it should be supplemented by anyone in the meeting who wants to contribute additional information. In this phase you should be alert to challenge the factual value of every statement. You can ask, "Do you know this of your own personal knowledge?" Or, "On what do you base this statement?" Opinions should be ruthlessly labeled as such. If the facts are too numerous or complex to be carried in mind, it's worth while to tabulate them on a blackboard.

4. Allow anyone to challenge these "facts" if he desires. Here you may get opinions which should be given weight as opinion—e.g., people may question whether there is enough evidence to accept some of the "facts" or whether other essential knowledge is lacking. If this is serious, the group may see that the meeting should adjourn to allow time for verifying or supplementing the facts. But if the group will agree on the facts, you're ready for the next step.

5. Clarify the question. It may be, "Under these circumstances,

what shall we do?" Or, the narrower one, "Shall we, or shall we not?"

6. If it simmers down to a choice between a few clear courses of action, have the group debate them. Limitation of the length of speeches is a must. If possible you should try to give the floor to proponents of each course in turn. Certainly you shouldn't let a speaker have the floor a second time if it is requested by anyone who hasn't yet been heard. When everyone who wants to talk has had his alloted time, you should have no trouble in putting the question to a vote.

7. However, if there are no clear-cut choices, but a wide variety of possible actions, you'll save time by the "brainstorming" technique. Let everyone make single-sentence suggestions, which are listed on a blackboard as fast as offered. Nobody can argue or object to a suggestion until all proposals are listed. No proposal, however weird, is refused listing.

8. Vote on every suggestion listed—not to settle the course of action, but to see how many people want the suggestion discussed further. Anyone may vote for as many different suggestions as he chooses. Tabulate the number of votes for each.

9. Obviously a big group can't thoroughly discuss a half-dozen good suggestions within reasonable time limits. The solution is to divide into small subgroups. Each subgroup should have six to eight members, should be a cross-section of various factions, and should be assigned to discuss one of the various proposals. After about a half-hour it should be ready to make a succinct report, in writing, of the advantages and disadvantages of the plan it discussed.

Each of these subgroups (often called buzz groups in social work) should promptly select one person as chairman and another as secretary. During the time allotted every member must be given a chance to speak for or against the suggestion, and to describe any ideas he has for putting it into effect or improving it. The secretary should take careful notes of every point made.

In this way, every suggestion which has much backing can get thoroughly aired. If sixty people are present, they can form as many as ten subgroups; ten suggestions will probably be the maximum number which win large votes during the polling in step 8 above. If there are fewer suggestions than there are subgroups, simply assign the leading suggestions to two groups for simultaneous discussion. It will be interesting to compare their reports.

10. At the end of the time allotted for subgroup discussion, call together the whole assemblage once more. The secretary of each subgroup now makes his report. He should speak no longer than two or three minutes.

11. If only one course of action must be decided on, take a series of ballots. After each ballot, eliminate the idea with the fewest votes. Thus your final vote will be between the two surviving plans. This balloting should usually be done without further discussion, since the arguments for and against each plan have presumably been stated in the subgroup reports. If you decide to permit arguments during this stage of the meeting, you'll want to get advance agreement to a time limit.

12. Now comes the final step: organization.

If your mass meeting is to produce anything but a lot of talk, it must end in the acceptance by individuals of concrete assignments to do something. Once a plan of action is agreed on, you're justified in assuming that its strongest advocates, at least, stand ready to carry it out. So you'll either appoint a steering committee to organize mass action, or you'll conduct an election of temporary officers, or you'll appoint various committees to do whatever jobs are indicated.

What steps you take will depend on the project itself. In any case, you should see to it that your meeting results in (a) agreement by the group as to action to be taken, and (b) acceptance by individuals of responsibility for the agreed-on action.

CHAPTER 8

The Curse of the
Absent Committeemen

Couldn't they come—or wouldn't they?

"WHEN I get a notice of a committee meeting," says Mr. Henry P. Hiatus, who belongs to many committees, "I sometimes decide not to go—either because I can't, or I don't want to. If the latter, it's either because I'm not interested or I want to do something else. If the former, it's either because I have something more important on tap, or I want to do something more pleasant or entertaining. In the rare cases when I want to do something more pleasant it's because . . ."

And so on. Mr. Hiatus always finds a logical, well-thought-out reason for his many absences.

So do we all. Being noble souls, rational and non-lazy, we have a good reason whenever we decide to skimp one of our civic duties. On the other hand, we somehow find time for whatever we really want to do.

Sparsely attended meetings baffle and pain many a committee chairman. Of all the problems that beset a businessman in civic service, this is one of the commonest. Perhaps he shrugs and tells himself, "It was bad luck. Things came up to keep a lot of people away."

This may be true—if an influenza epidemic is raging. Illness does occasionally keep people away from meetings. But if anything else—anything at all—keeps them away, hadn't the chairman better ask himself if he could have done something to get them there?

Henry P. Hiatus, and thousands like him, never tell a chairman that they stayed away from his meeting by choice. Yet if the meeting had been made more attractive or convenient, they would have come.

It simmers down to this. Absence is always due to (a) physical disability or (b) lack of interest or (c) conflict with other interests. Either of the latter two causes—which cover about 99% of the absences—calls for remedial action by any chairman worthy of his chair.

If they couldn't, do this

If you were dealing with truants on your payroll, you'd take one course of action. If you faced a rebellious platoon under your military command, you might take various others. But those straight, stern moves are closed to you now. You're dealing with your friends. You have no power to compel attendance at committee meetings.

You may think people slack or wrong-headed for staying away. But they have other interests. Why must they give priority to your committee?

A smart chairman knows that Dave goes to church Wednesday evenings; that Bob's wife hates to be left alone in the house after ten p.m.; that Al bowls on Fridays; that Horace has to get up at five a.m. to drive to work; that Pete reserves week ends to take his family to their cabin.

Therefore he tries hard not to call a meeting for a time which will automatically keep away some members. And he is adroit in adjusting to their habits and tastes. Perhaps he arranges for them to bring their spouses for a social evening while the committee is in session. Perhaps he suggests they might prefer to meet oftener, say for dinner and an hour afterward, than to put in a full evening at longer intervals. Perhaps he finds that a breakfast meeting would suit everyone better; it often would, especially in smaller cities, where offices may be only a few minutes away from a breakfast table.

By careful checking and planning, you'll solve most problems of your absentees who chronically can't come. The problem is really yours, if you fix the time for the meeting. Set a time acceptable to them, and you'll get better attendance.

Of course you're still left with the problem of people like Henry Hiatus, who sometimes just don't want to come. We turn next to them.

Whose fault if they wouldn't?

The fine art of chairmanship includes attention to subtleties which seem trivial—such as the choice of a meeting place. Is it easily reached? Is it comfortable? Is it acceptable?

Why huddle in a church basement if members would be more at ease in your parlor? Or why drive miles to somebody's home if a downtown office would be handier?

Will committee members want to smoke? If so, the chairman keeps it in mind. He doesn't pick a place where smoking may be taboo. And he's aware that the parlor of a Christian Science family, or some Baptist or Mormon households, may fall in this category. At any rate, he makes sure beforehand.

A large committee sometimes has trouble locating a big enough meeting room. Then it discovers a community church which seems to fit nicely. But the smart chairman remembers that Catholics are reluctant to meet in a Protestant church even to discuss a get-out-the-vote campaign. He checks with his members on such questions.

If his committee meets for a meal, he gives thought to what the members like to eat and how much they prefer to pay. If Mr. Hiatus hates highly spiced food he'll shun a meeting at La Cucaracha Mexicana. But the right food at the right price may lure him even when he has reason to be elsewhere.

The chairman's art also includes starting meetings on time. In a poorly run committee, emphatic announcements may be made that the meeting will start on the dot; but anyone who takes these at face value finds himself waiting. Such meetings will start later and later—not because of the chairman's tardiness, but because members have been taught to discount his announcements. They deliberately arrive late.

No doubt he hopes he'll have a better meeting if he delays "until more people get here." But the devoted souls who came on time will secretly disagree with him. They wonder, *Are these other people so much more necessary than I?* And they wonder, *Who knows whether they're really coming at all?*

In the long run you're always better off to start on time. The few who are punctual, perhaps at some sacrifice, will appreciate it The late arrivals won't feel aggrieved, though they may be embarrassed. The agenda will be covered sooner, and with less haste. Naturally you'll plan your agenda so the most important items come up toward mid-meeting, after the stragglers arrive but before anyone starts yawning.

Beyond avoiding these small irritants, the artful chairman tries to make sure that members will feel his meetings are productive. He takes care to have all needed information and materials on hand. He keeps discussion moving toward its specific, stated objectives. He hates, fears, and guards determinedly against do-nothing meetings—because he knows that only a few of these will wipe out most of a committee's membership no matter how comfortable the chairs, how delicious the dinner, how carefully chosen the time and place.

But was it all the chairman's fault?

Since the chairman is the steersman, the foregoing suggestions were beamed at him. But presumably the committee members will feel responsibility too. It's their committee as well as his. When you're a committeeman rather than chairman, shouldn't you alert the chairman if you see hazards which he doesn't?

If he didn't deduce that your new dentures made the last steak dinner impossible for you, let him know, before he repeats. If you've heard members grumble because smoking wasn't permissible, tell him—and suggest a meeting place that would satisfy everyone.

If he called a meeting for a time which kept you and others away, he'll appreciate being told. Yes, he should have inquired, but since he didn't why leave him in the dark? You're all friends.

If you offer it without any air of personal carping, almost any chairman will welcome and act on a friendly suggestion that can improve attendance at his meetings. You as a member ought to make such suggestions, since you're there to help. This isn't one of those times when "least said, soonest mended."

Come-hither by mail

As we've seen, dwindling attendance usually means that committee members were displeased with previous meetings. Their displeasure is usually traceable to the chairman's errors.

The conscientious chairman will not only maneuver to avoid those errors in future, but will let his members know this. His letter can point out winsomely that a better time or place has been chosen. More important, it should show a worthy, interesting reason for holding the next meeting. Lack of visible reason for a meeting causes lack of attendance.

The average meeting is heralded dully as "a meeting to consider future plans," or something equally vague—or duller yet, as the regular monthly meeting; end of message. A form announcement is a deadly weapon for driving away all but the determined members.

Why not use a touch of showmanship when you summon your committee? One touch is to send an advance copy of the agenda, laden with as much dynamite as you dare. Make it sound arresting, even ominous if the facts justify. "What shall we do about the fire hazards in the club building?" is a more suspenseful agenda topic than "Maintenance Problems."

If the agenda can't be announced, because of diplomatic reasons or incomplete plans, you might at least send a notice mentioning a prickly topic or two which will come up at the meeting. You waste postage if you merely write, "There are several important matters to be discussed." Specify them.

One Elks committee, working on plans for a new building, slogged through a series of rather routine meetings with full attendance because the astute chairman pointed up some problem in each invitation; here is a typical statement: "There appears to be a serious difference of opinion whether we should recommend a well-equipped kitchen, or plan to build now without it and add it later."

Another chairman's note got his camp committee agog: "We have been offered a donation to pay for installing a rifle range at camp. But there have been objections to our having rifles in camp. We must let the prospective donor know at once whether we can accept his offer." All pro-gun and anti-gun members came to the meeting.

Sometimes in a crisis it's better to be cryptic than frank. For example, the chairman of one junior baseball club found that parents weren't providing enough transportation to haul the club to away-from-home games. Instead of a reproachful SOS to parents to "discuss the transportation shortage," which might have kept some away, he sent each family a personal note which said only:

> A serious situation has arisen affecting your son's membership in the club. There will be a meeting to discuss it at my home next Monday at 7:30 p.m. I hope you can come, because I cannot undertake to explain the situation by phone.

The parents came as if extradited. And when he laid the problem in their laps—more dramatically and convincingly than he could have by mail—he got the needed automobiles.

When you send advance copies of an agenda, usually the best bet is to make it only a skeleton of the real working agenda, so you can play up the provocative topics. Each copy can carry a penned notation to its recipient, about any specific items on which you need his report or advice.

Here's a sample skeleton agenda sent to members of a finance campaign team. You'll notice that it makes clear the meeting time, promises members help with their difficulties, and titillates them on a subject which is a bone of contention:

12:30 Lunch (steak sandwiches)
        Collect report envelopes

1:00 Reports on difficult prospects who will be taken over by Flying Squadron

1:15 Announcement of decision by C. of C. regarding exceptions to rule against employee solicitations

1:30 Decision regarding additional quotas in light of C. of C.'s concessions

        Agree on date and place of next meeting

2:30 Adjourn

On each copy was some penned note to each individual: "Tom, I'd like you to tell briefly how you got that $50 from Duxall Co. . . . Bill, this is the time to turn in that $75 from the Mothers Club . . ."

They don't need me tonight

You can't always magnetize Henry P. Hiatus with an intriguing announcement of an urgent reason for meeting. Mr. Hiatus, being normal, is often a vicitim of inertia. It's easy for him to think, "Well, these are hot topics on the agenda, but the other members can handle them. They'll tell me later what happened. They don't particularly need me tonight."

Therefore a chairman's job of wooing each of the many Messrs. Hiatus doesn't end with showing that the meeting is momentous. Every in-and-outer must see the necessity for his personal presence. The careful chairman will make sure he does see.

If Mr. Hiatus is on a team of fund solicitors, he can be reminded that "You'll want to come and pick out the names of prospects you prefer to solicit." Or that he is needed "to explain to the new members how you handled that Duxall situation."

If the committee is to inspect campsites, the chairman may tell Henry, "I'd hate to have the committee make a decision until we know which site you think has the best waterfront possibilities." Or, when the chairman can't think of any more personal appeal, he may say, "I'd appreciate it if you'd pick up Cal and Jim, to make the transportation easier."

Having one member pick up others is a good idea any time, especially when they must travel some distance. Most people dislike a long, lonesome drive. By pooling cars, some members are coaxed out who might otherwise find reasons to stay away.

This is one more of the standard stratagems a chairman can try on everybody. Ease of transportation, like a comfortable meeting room and a good meal, will tip the scales sometimes. All the same, Henry Hiatus will almost certainly go to the most Spartan gathering if he knows that he is important to it. He's a good-hearted chap or he wouldn't be in community work. When he's sure he's needed, he'll come.

Therefore ask yourself as chairman: Why is Henry needed at this meeting? What can and should he contribute to it? How can I appeal to his personal pride, his sense of duty, or his desire to see a certain issue decided the "right" way?

Each member of a committee was enlisted for a reason. There were specific ways he could help. Remind him of this whenever you call a meeting—so he can seldom tell himself, "They'll get along just as well without me."

The wrong kind of reminder

After mailing your meeting announcements, you might well use still another lure to promote attendance: check with each member a few hours before the meeting.

Some chairmen think: "Why remind these people again? They've had written notice. They're adults. If they want to come they'll come, without nagging from me."

This sounds logical. But it doesn't make for well-attended meetings. People do overlook engagements sometimes. And they do misunderstand sometimes, no matter how clearly worded the chairman's notice. If a member has an important role to play, a diligent chairman will want to make sure he hasn't been stricken ill or called away. Hence the check-up.

Consider the angry confusion which arose in the altar committee of one church. A member left town because of a daughter's illness. Due notice was given to the chairman, who duly phoned an alternate to fill in for the coming Sunday. The alternate agreed, and was reminded by postcard.

On that Sunday the alternate served as specified, and thought no more of it. The original arrangements had been made by phone, so she scarcely glanced at the confirming postcard—which stated explicitly that she was needed for the remainder of the month.

Consequently, on the second Sunday she came to church as usual and sat in the congregation. The books were not set out on the lectern, or the flowers arranged around the altar. To the furious chairman this seemed inexcusable. But the alternate, a most conscientious lady, felt that since she was an alternate she was expected to serve only when asked. Just an innocent misunderstanding. But it caused a failure of altar service, and hot words between friends. A phone call would have averted all the anguish.

Yes, eleventh-hour check-ups by phone are worth the effort. But don't leave them to the hired help.

The paid staff of a volunteer organization probably has many meetings a week to drum up. It's all the staff can do, usually, to send postcards. If superhumanly diligent, they may also ask an office girl to phone and remind the members (or their secretaries). But persuasion or elucidation is beyond them.

If Henry Hiatus is undecided, the mimeographed form card and the perfunctory phone reminder are just what he needs to convince him that this is just another routine meeting. They may keep him away when he had previously planned to attend.

This is especially true if Henry has missed the last couple of meetings. He'll be irritated by such an impersonal reminder. It shows that nobody cares much whether he comes or goes; if it had mattered, someone would have taken more pains to urge him.

As chairman, you want him there. Convince him. But more important, try to make sure that he himself will want to come. When in doubt, you may need to use your influence, and your salesmanship. Phone him personally. If you can't reach him, and you truly want him at your meeting, then put on your hat and go to see him. Personal calls are the best convincers.

What to say when you call

But your visit or phone call will be wasted if you say no more than, "Hope you'll be at the meeting." Be emphatic. Be specific. Above all, be genuine. He is important, and you have to show him why he is.

Unless he were really needed, you wouldn't go to all this bother. Since he is needed, you can tell him in all sincerity, "Henry, it's essential that you come. There'll be an argument about this Spelvin matter. Your insight is important to us. There'll be questions asked that only you can answer properly."

Or you can lay out some part of the agenda as his personal chore, such as "explaining which prospects should be turned over to the Flying Squadron, and why." Or ask him to "clarify the position of the Community Chest on solicitation by agencies." Ask him to be the spokesman in favor of accepting the donation for the rifle range—or against it, if that's his position.

Before you invite a waverer to a meeting, plan his role. Presumably you don't try to avoid arguments about controversial questions which come before your committee. You want the committee to do what's right, whether its decision agrees with your own view or not. To reach the right decision, the committee needs the unique contribution of each of its diverse members.

Each member, then, has a significant role. Explain it to him. If he really can't come, perhaps you'll want to ask him to send a substitute, even if it means using an outsider. Insist that the job must be done!

A trick for taking roll

In a big committee a chairman or secretary sometimes calls the roll orally, or passes a blank sheet for everyone to sign. In a small committee, the names are silently jotted down for the minutes.

Either way, the committee is missing a good bet for promoting attendance. It could use the roll-taking for what psychologists call peer pressure. Each man can be silently made aware that he's losing face in the eyes of his peers if his attendance is poor.

To do this, simply make a permanent record sheet for the year, or for the life of the committee, with names of all members and a dated column for each meeting. Pass the sheet around at each meeting, asking every member to put his initials opposite his name in that meeting's column.

Thus everyone sees everyone else's attendance record. An irregular member knows his absence won't go unnoticed. His history of faithfulness or delinquence will be apparent at each meeting.

No comment is needed. He'll soon be discomfited into getting busy or giving up his place to someone in better position to fill it.

After the meeting, two tricks

1. Follow up, systematically but suavely, on absentees. The chairman needn't handle this alone. Others may do some of it better than he. Whoever does it, the reason why Mr. Hiatus was absent should concern the others.

The chairman or a committeeman can phone in the friendliest fashion to say that everyone missed him; you thought he'd want to know what happened at the meeting, so you're calling to tell him. Sometimes the conversation is shaped so that Mr. Hiatus volunteers for, or at least accepts, some work arising out of the committee's deliberations. This provides leverage for getting him to the next meeting.

The impact on Henry is even more staggering if several members tell him how sadly they needed him at the meeting. No kidding. It's no use asking, "How was the show last Tuesday while we slaved at the meeting?" Nor will he be stricken to hear that he missed a good dinner. But he will be rather dashed if members express sober regret that their mutual project was hampered by his absence. This is another instance of peer pressure. It works.

2. Everyone, present or strayed, should receive a report of the meeting. Not the detailed minutes—just a fast summary, with a line or two for each action taken. Append a list showing who was there, who wasn't. If you know the ostensible reason for an absence, put it on the record. If the meeting decided that certain members would do specific jobs, let the summary show this clearly, as reminder and prod. Here's how:

Present:	Dan Mills	Absent:	Ted Pingree (in N.Y. on
	Clyde Peaslee		business)
	Lester Dawes		Dick Dayton (date made
	Mark Dean		by his wife)
	Myron Scott		

WE MET under Dan's chairmanship, in the absence of Chairman Ted.

WE REVIEWED our first-quarter record: 4 Packs, 5 Troops, 7 Explorer Posts organized to date—a 50% increase over last year's first quarter. All districts except Central have organized new units this year.

WE AGREED to include basic training as a part of unit organization from now on.

and to distribute the pamphlet "The First Month" gratis when needed, paying for it out of the committee's budget.

WE ACCEPTED ASSIGNMENTS as follows:

Clyde to contact First Congregational Church
Les and Mark to put on basic training for new Kiwanis troop
Myron to meet troop committee of 19 and help them reorganize

WE ENJOYED Mrs. Mills' excellent pumpkin pie and coffee before adjourning at 10:15.

As another follow-up you may want to mail complete minutes shortly before the next meeting—especially if there was deep and weighty discussion. If you do, make sure that chairman and secretary agree as to the accuracy of the record. (See "Danger! Secretary at Work" in Chapter 10.)

CHAPTER 9

Welcome to the Board Meeting

> *It takes four years to get a new idea across*
> *to a board of directors.*
> —CHARLES F. KETTERING

The art of throwing monkey wrenches

Now WE CLIMB into the upper atmosphere of volunteer work: the rarefied and rocky region where the Board sits.

By "board" we mean primarily the group of elected or appointed trustees who set high policy and oversee the work of an organization devoted to social betterment—such groups as school boards and alumni councils, church vestries, the hierarchy of a lodge, the directorate of a service club or veterans' organization, the executive board of a casework or group work agency or a health or charitable organization.

However, this chapter likewise fits any standing committee which supervises an "expert"—the casework committee of an adoption agency, for example, or the program committee of a Boys' Club; even a troop committee or a district committee in Scouting, though they supervise nonprofessional Scoutmasters and district commissioners (who display many of the virtues and faults of paid headmen).

As Lewis Mumford points out in *The Conduct of Life*, "Groups become sluggish and automatic in their behavior, incapable of making fresh decisions, like persons." This is why groups such as boards need new members such as you. Constant re-examination of their assumptions is needed—and you should be one of the examiners.

Of course your examination will be silent for a while. You'll educate yourself by asking mental questions: Why must we do it this way? Is there a better way? Why do it at all? What isn't being done that should be? Are our end-results worth while? Are we taking too much for granted? Are we looking far enough ahead?

Sometimes a little thought or research will show you valid reasons for a doctrine which looked invalid at first glance. On the other hand, your fresh eyes may see what older ones don't. The common joke, "There's no reason for it, it's just our policy," is funny because it often is true.

When you think you can suggest an improvement, sound out some members privately. Ease around to your suggestion circumspectly: "What are the reasons for this? Does everyone agree on the facts? Have we ever considered different methods? What would be the pros and cons of trying such and such?"

You're unlikely to get three cheers for any inquiry which hints that the old way isn't best. People tend to resist change. Regardless of the make-up of a board, it will resent any newcomer who loudly challenges the Establishment; on the other hand it will certainly be tolerant of questions—even foolish questions— by a new colleague who asks with tact and humility. Therefore your first concern, if you would be an effective board member, should be to inform yourself without treading too heavily on anyone's toes at the first few meetings.

The board may answer your questions with a stout defense of the status quo, and perhaps you can only say, "Thanks, I'm glad to be set straight," but at least you've done a service by nudging the board into thinking about its position. If you're still skeptical of its thinking, you can find diplomatic ways to reopen the question from other angles at future meetings.

It takes time, but in the long run the cheery motto of Beardsley Ruml holds true: "Reasonable men always agree if they understand what they are talking about." To reach understanding and agreement, try to get facts instead of opinions. As Bertrand Russell pointed out, the heat of one's emotion varies inversely with one's knowledge of the facts. The less people know about a subject, the hotter they get while discussing it.

There are some good semantic devices to help cool down a hot verbal clash. Instead of stating a fact bluntly, it helps to start with the phrase, "As far as I know . . ." and when you want to express disagreement, you can meet your opponent halfway by beginning, "Up to a point, you are probably right in saying—" and then, after repeating his statement in his own words, you can show where you think it goes wrong. This same device works well in reverse; when you want to express an opinion (if you must resort to it, instead of relying on facts) you can phrase it as a question—"Up to what point would I be right in saying . . . ?"

After you've served a while on a board, you can and should ask more questions. J. C. Baker says in *Directors and Their Functions*:

> The most effective directors, by general agreement, are those who ask the most discerning questions. "The foreknowledge that searching questions will be asked is a psychological barrier to the proposal of half-baked projects," to quote one vice-president.

The feeling that you know less about an organization than its front-line workers and headquarters specialists shouldn't deter you from questioning (albeit cautiously and sympathetically) a policy or practice which looks unwise to you. Harold Laski remarked reasonably enough: "Although the plain man doesn't understand the principles of highway engineering, he certainly is capable of making judgments about the quality of the road over which he drives his car."

Better backslapping

All groups considered here as boards are supervising the work of someone else—a professional or volunteer "expert"—who in turn gives advice to the board. He recommends actions to be taken by the board or by the rank-and-file under its banner. You'll recognize, then, that when you ask questions in board meetings (as we urged in the previous section) you are probably challenging something the expert either has advised or has tacitly accepted.

Don't put your expert on the defensive unnecessarily. If he feels you are criticizing him, he will react as most of us do when someone questions our professional competence. Although he may be urbane enough to conceal it even from himself, he'll feel a bit hostile.

Your mission is to help him. If you antagonize him, he's less willing to be helped. Furthermore, you lose influence and prestige with the board if you seem to be a chronic objector or a bull in a china shop.

You can easily phrase your questions to show the staff man that you're on his side, that you respect him, that you're sure he has weighty reasons for whatever has been done. If there's a need for improvement, try to make him think he suggested it himself. And whenever he deserves praise, dish it up.

Remember that managing any kind of welfare organization is hectic work. The staff badly needs cheering from time to time. Professional social workers hear plenty of complaints, woefully little applause. They often feel undervalued by their own board people, "who feel culturally vindicated and politically elite," as one resentful social worker put it.

Intelligent backslapping, therefore, is desirable at board meetings. Try to show the professional that you understand and appreciate what he is doing. Restate and endorse his views when you agree with them. Treat him as a worthy partner. (In Chapter 11 we'll try to give you more insight into how he thinks, feels, and operates.)

When you have misgivings about a board tenet, and can't find reassurance in informal talks with well-informed members, then it's often good practice to put your questions privately to the professional. If he satisfies you, as he usually will, he'll be pleased and you'll be saved embarrassment at the meeting. If you still disagree, there's no need to hide it, but you can at least be good-natured about your differences.

Even when you're sure the professional is demonstrably wrong, velvet gloves are better than brass knuckles. Possibly if you're adroit enough he'll see the need of your counsel and seek it. If not, you may win a victory but lose a war by telling him that "some of the trustees are critical of your ideas," or by arraigning him at the board table. He might resign in a huff, or his defenders could spring at your throat, or other upheavals could occur, causing grave damage to the organization.

A smoother approach is through some board member who is the professional's trusted friend. This intermediary can quietly show him the objections to the old order, and enlist his help in changing it; can suggest taking advantage of "the valuable background of some of the board," which can turn out to mean consulting you. Most administrators jump at the chance to consult board members who seem likely to be useful and friendly.

The sensitive grass roots

Few boards are very perceptive in their treatment of another spirited and thin-skinned group of people: the volunteer corps. This is one reason why many organizations have a high turnover among their low-echelon volunteers.

Those obscure warriors who man the ramparts are in some ways more important to your movement than you are. The solicitors who ring doorbells in fund drives; the teachers who actually face the pupils; the Cubmasters and coaches and choir directors; the regular working membership of the PTA and Kiwanis and Masonry and all the rest—they often slave harder for a cause, dig deeper into their pockets, and take more punishment than any board member does.

They may resent you. Possibly you're a come-lately while they are seasoned campaigners. They see you taking bows at banquets and rallies, but they seldom see the work you do. They suspect that you know less, and care less, about the organization than they do.

Every board should try to bestow status symbols on its unsung heroes at the base of the pyramid. If you pick a Man of the Year, must he be a board member? Whenever some liegeman achieves greatly, can't he be honored conspicuously? Does your board show any appreciation of the indispensable work done every day in the dim lower depths?

Of course the dedicated stalwarts down there don't really care whether the board gives them medals and publicity. They find fulfillment in the service they perform. But if they regard you as their appreciative backers, rather than as a remote mysterious cabal of grandees, you can weld them into a more understanding and cooperative team.

Fish for their comments and suggestions. In some of the strongest service clubs, each board member makes a point of sitting beside different non-board members each week. He tells them he needs guidance from the membership; he asks their opinion of board actions. He listens, and learns.

Every board should be on guard against seeming to look down on its constituency. When the chairman of a hospital board remarked to the women's auxiliary, "We've worked out new plans, but information won't get down to your level for several months yet," his lordly phrase was widely quoted and remembered. After plans did filter down they fell on deaf ears.

Wherever friends are to be won, wherever support is to be strengthened, board members should be good-will ambassadors. They can open doors which may be closed to other people. Unfortunately they sometimes close doors too. It cost Harvard University thirty-four million dollars because a trustee snubbed a shabby couple who visited him. They asked how much it cost to run a university. He thought their question was impertinent and silly, so he got rid of them quickly. Instead of giving Harvard the money, as they had planned, the Leland Stanfords returned to California and founded their own university.

In his book *Building Up Your Congregation,* adman William Pleuthner warns of "the dangerous dignity of church boards." The same warning might apply to many other kinds of social work boards. One of their chief weaknesses, according to Pleuthner, is that they have too many bankers, lawyers, doctors and retired corporate executives, and too few "sales managers, advertising men, and active business executives on the way up the ladder." What does he find wrong with bankers and lawyers? They "achieved success by having people come to them for help, and not by going out and selling their services to people who needed them."

Good communication both upward and downward is especially useful when policy changes or new projects are in the works. A financial setback threatened the Boy Scout organization in Los

Angeles because its Scoutmasters were lukewarm about selling tickets to its annual big show. But board members hastily gave a series of district dinners for Scoutmasters—not to exhort them to sell tickets, but to ask their counsel. Should the show be continued? Should its proceeds be invested on the proposed improvements of Scout camps, or would the Scoutmasters recommend other improvements instead?

The resulting interchange not only enlightened the board and helped it improve the project, but also enlighted the Scoutmasters and enthused them about the show. It was now their project as much as the board's. They went forth to sell thousands of tickets.

Another useful service a board can render is to find ways to make the work of the volunteers easier and pleasanter. In some of the big voluntary organizations a front-line worker feels like a man standing under an avalanche. He gets questionnaires, check lists, score sheets, agenda, minutes, manuals, mandates, monographs, announcements, warnings, invitations, petitions, proclamations, corrections, suggestions, pep letters and postcards by the pound. Can your board cut the number of mailings? Make them more readable or useful? If volunteer training is necessary, can you take it to them instead of importuning them to travel long distances for it?

When you schedule meetings for your volunteers, remember that you're asking busy people to leave fireside and family. Inviting them to bring along their wives, and providing diversion for the ladies while the men are occupied, makes attendance more agreeable and meetings more successful.

Hard as it is from such a height, board members must try to keep their eyes on the grass roots. Perhaps the paramount duty of a board is to help its field workers to be effective.

Beware of the staff

There is a sentence in a book on social agencies that reads: "As social agencies grow larger they tend to withdraw from their constituency." First of all, given a job that involves both field work and desk work, the tendency is to gravitate more to the desk. Second, there is the tendency to serve the success rather than the failure, to attend the banquet of the successful unit rather than setting up a meeting to reorganize the unsuccessful one. Third, there is the tendency to spend less time showing how, and more time telling how—and the larger the audience, the better. Withdrawal is a beguiling trap. The big job that needs doing is still in the units, in the neighborhood, in the district.

The above warning, in a regional newsletter for Scout executives, is worth heeding by board members too. Any social agency board must be alert for signs of "withdrawal" by its staff, and perhaps by itself. Yet it must also guard against overinvolvement by the staff; a manager who does everything himself is as dangerous as one who does nothing.

The relationship between board and staff is odd. A standing joke among professional staff workers is that their job is "to tell the people who hire me what they should have me do."

This is true enough, at least in matters of technical know-how. The staff has deeper knowledge of the philosophy on which the organization is founded, and of mistakes and successes elsewhere; so the staff is hired to give the volunteers the benefit of its knowledge.

But the trustees, not the staff, are the true bosses. The board rules the organization, holds the purse strings, hires and fires the professionals.

In watching the staff, how can a board know what to look for? How can it judge whether the staff is competent? Where is the line between decisions the board should make and decisions it should leave to its employees?

An analogy may be helpful. Suppose you were in a town devastated by flood or fire. You and other volunteers might scrape up money and hire a professional camp cook to manage the feeding of the homeless populace. You would not expect him to do the actual cooking for the town, would you? His job would be to supervise a corps of volunteer cooks recruited by you; to work out menus and quantities; to make the best possible use of whatever foods and equipment you procured for him. Raising money to pay for all this would be the community's responsibility, not his.

Yet some boards expect their executive to run a one-man show: to find the money, plan the activities, recruit the volunteers, make all the decisions and handle all the hot potatoes. Some old-fashioned welfare executives try to do just this.

This type of staff is inclined to treat a board member "like a courtier handling an idiot monarch who has absolute power but no sense," in the words of Marion K. Sanders. And the staff may settle into comfortable lifetime ruts, if the board waives responsibility as critics, policymakers, movers and shakers.

Many board members are diffident and docile in the presence of a professional staff person. They need to be reminded of *The Limitations of the Expert*, as delineated by Harold Laski:

> The expert tends to sacrifice the insight of common sense to the intensity of his experience.
> The expert dislikes the appearance of novel views.
> The expert too often fails to see his results in proper perspective.
> The expert may develop a dangerous caste spirit.
> The expert is so immersed in routine that he lacks flexibility of mind outside his special field.
> The expert frequently tends to develop a condescension toward the plain man.

Analytic comprehension of a special realm of facts is purchased at the cost of the kind of wisdom essential to the conduct of affairs.

The expert tends to push his private cures for social ills without reference to popular wants and desires. He mistakes technical results for social wisdom.

Too frequently the expert dismisses the plain man as ignorant and incapable of having legitimate judgment or point of view.

This of course does not argue that it is therefore wise to appoint non-experts as executives, to protect the public from zealous experts in our agencies.

The above seems a staggering list of faults, and Professor Laski did well to add his final sentence. Granted that many experts are lost outside their own field, they are invaluable guides within it. You need only be careful to keep a sharp lookout when you serve on a board. You were asked to be a trustee because you have wider perspective than the expert. Use your eyes and your judgment.

—and beware of yourself

"We all know the unfortunate reputation of charitable institutions," says a character in Louis Auchincloss' novel, *The Great World and Timothy Colt*. "How they are supposed to take the nickel out of the beggar's cup to swell the coffers of their own wards. How they recognize no poverty or distress outside the categories of their own charters. I have always sought to check this tendency in the charity boards on which I have sat."

Many a board shows this human impulse toward clannishness. Some Boy Scout enthusiasts view Little Leaguers as the powers of darkness. The Cancer Society may think a United Fund is the work of wreckers. One adoption agency spreads talk that another adoption agency's fees are outrageous.

As a board member, you must help the organization rise above sectarianism. The professionals and the regular volunteers are more likely than you to become zealots.

But clannishness is only one of many faults to which board members may fall prey. Here is a capsule summary of other human failings seen sometimes at board meetings: clock-watching; table-pounding; rubber-stamping reports of committees or staff; yessing old buddies; harping on pet peeves or cure-alls; pressing for hasty decisions; wandering off the subject; viewing with too much alarm; and pointing with too much pride.

These and other pitfalls at the board table are given extended treatment in a valuable book by Roy Sorenson, *The Art of Board Membership*. You'll find it useful in recognizing both helpful and harmful behavior in yourself and other board members. Meanwhile, take a hard look at your own habits in the board room. Few of us are above reproach there.

CHAPTER 10

Some Problems of Presidents

Why many boards decay

> The principal business at nearly every board meeting should be the report of the executive and members of the staff. It is largely through the medium of such reports that board members become familiar with the work of the agency and keep in touch with it. Matters of ordinary business routine should be handled with all possible dispatch so that ample time will be available for these reports.

THE ABOVE, from a manual for board members published by a social-welfare organization, is gospel to many social workers—and anathema to businessmen. Sitting in board meetings merely to hear reports does not jibe with their ideas of how to use their time.

Yet the statement, if wisely interpreted, can be a sound guide for any board. Only far-gone longhairs take it to mean that the "principal business" should be an edifying report from the staff, followed by earnest but unimportant palaver and then adjournment. This is the kind of meeting which drives out board members. Trustees of stature quickly conclude that the staff has everything in hand and that they can be more useful elsewhere.

Correctly interpreted, the statement at the head of the chapter implies that the board will receive reports in order to act on them.

A staff report should not be a list of achievements or recital of unenlightening statistics. It should be information about changes which call for policymaking, for allocating or raising funds, for correcting misinterpretations—and so on. In other words, because of a report a board should make a decision.

A president or board chairman should make sure that the agenda of his meeting (which he normally works out in advance with the paid executive) will include reports to be used as springboards for action. If it is the right kind of board, it will want always to see some big plans progressing from month to month.

Certainly "matters of ordinary business routine should be handled with all possible dispatch," as the welfare manual advises. Unless such matters *are* handled by the board, someone lower down might feel free to do things which the board wouldn't approve if it knew. For example, disbursements outside the approved budget, even if obviously justified, usually require board approval. Some boards require that they be informed whenever there are changes in staff personnel. This takes a little time, but it guards against misjudgment or injustice inside the secretariat. Letters of complaint, if addressed to the board or the president, should be read at board meetings so that no brewing trouble can be hidden by a staff member.

These matters are routine in the sense that very little discussion is needed unless a board member senses something wrong. Normally they can and should be approved with dispatch. A board which wastes its time niggling over trivia is on the road to decay.

After routine is disposed of, the trustees have a right to expect a clear and complete (but concise) view of the state of the organization, and "a brightening vision of its future," as the president emeritus of Albion College phrased it, so they can help meet its short-range and long-range needs. Sometimes a staff, unless guided and quizzed by a president, is too close to details to realize what kind of reports are needed.

Many men with solid business background but brief experience on civic boards are chiefly interested in the operating statement of the institution. They want to know whether the budget is balanced. This is a good starting point. Myron F. Wicke points out in *Handbook for Trustees:*

> There are many instances on record in which boards of trustees were astonished to learn that the institution had been operating at a deficit, and that sizable indebtedness had developed. No board need be surprised by deficits when the reports of the president and business manager are clear and comprehensive, and when trustees ask the essential questions. Such questions should be raised. There can be no smoke screens between trustees and administration.

Still, full financial reports aren't enough. A human balance sheet as well as a fiscal one should be examined.

What is the enterprise accomplishing that justifies the toil and sacrifices of the people concerned with it? What quality, as well as quantity, of services does it render? The work of the organization is the sole reason for its existence, not the buttressing of budgets or the building of great plants, important as these may be.

Board members don't ordinarily expect to be given arduous missions in the field, but they do expect to be shown something to do. Presumably your organization has frontiers which ought to be pushed forward, or weak spots which need treatment. What are its major problems and opportunities, now and in the future? Keep your board aware of them. Ask its help and advice in safeguarding the standards of the movement, in reaching its goals, perhaps in adjusting its policies to a changing scene. Such basic tasks call into play the mental muscles which make a strong board.

The decay of a board—which simply means the loss of interest by its good members—is caused by the same condition which causes atrophy of bodily muscles: lack of use. Boards need challenges. It's up to presidents to make sure the challenges are visible.

Soporifics at the meeting

A time-honored time-waster in many board meetings is the "reading of the minutes of the last meeting." Everyone's attention strays while the secretary drones on. Theoretically the purpose is to bring everyone up to date, so business can resume from where it left off. But in practice this time is usually wasted.

Although minutes should be enlightening, they should not be read aloud (or even silently) at a meeting unless needed to throw light on some moot point. It's better to mail each trustee his personal copy—and even to invite him to mail or phone "any corrections or amendments" instead of calling for them at the next meeting.

When the board turns its attention to unfinished business, the president can briefly review the status of the business as he introduces it. Item by item, pending matters on the agenda can be quickly explained as they come up. Why sit through an unbroken exegesis of all these matters in one stupefying dose at the start of each meeting?

Another typical time-waster is the practice of self-introductions as a form of roll call or familiarization. If board members don't know each other, it's good practice to provide them with a typed sheet listing everyone's name and professional affiliation. Then as the president leads discussion he can make a point of addressing everyone by name, so that trustees can match up unfamiliar faces with names on their sheet.

Introduction of guests or new members is likewise a superfluous rigmarole for most boards. If introductions are needed, why not make them person-to-person before the meeting begins? Preliminary fraternizing with a newcomer is much more cordial than standing him up as an exhibit.

This same proceedure is the best kind of welcome for an outsider who has been invited to contribute his knowledge to some subject on the agenda. Time, we repeat, is of the essence. If his background is important, summarize it in a copy of the agenda given to every member, or put it in the preliminary notice of the meeting you mail to everyone.

Another breeder of boredom at board meetings is persiflage. A witty remark now and then can break tension or warm up a silent group. A genial presiding officer can sometimes lubricate progress. But there is danger in too much wit or geniality. Repeated bursts of laughter around the table may leave everyone in good humor, but sober second thoughts will set in afterward among the busier members of the board. How much did the repartee and story-telling slow down the agenda?

One of the president's problems is to curb comedians on his board. Sometimes he can do it with a good-natured grin and sharp rap of the gavel. Sometimes a playfully shaken finger will give the message. Sometimes he or a helpful colleague can cut in, "I'm laughing to pieces—but look at this long agenda. Can we get back to it?" There may be times when the only way to handle a persistent cut-up is for the president to catch him outside and set him straight.

Now and then we find trustees who insist that prolonging board meetings beyond the normal adjournment hour is necessary and worthwhile. In rare cases it may be. But consider the drawbacks.

Consider the reaction of the board member who told his secretary to expect him in the office at two o'clock, and returns at three to learn that he has missed an important caller. Consider the feelings of the trustee who must rise early the next morning after a board meeting which drags into the small hours.

Before you let a meeting run far overtime, weigh the importance of the board business against the importance of keeping faith with your board members. A farsighted president usually decides that keeping faith is more important. There are ways he can do justice to the agenda without trapping people into an unexpectedly long meeting.

If a question requires lengthy discussion, perhaps it can be studied in advance by small groups which can explain its ramifications tersely at the board meeting. If it is too urgent to be carried over until the next regular meeting, a special session can be scheduled at some time which won't do violence to members' other plans.

As one basic precaution, a president ought to look over the items on the program and estimate (a) the length of time each is likely to take, and (b) its importance.

Important items which threaten to stir up prolonged discussion should be introduced early, and unimportant items relegated to the bottom of the list so they can be put off until the next meeting if the hour grows late.

Another basic precaution is to hold the discussion firmly on the track. If a member takes off on a lengthy flight into side issues, there are various sharp remarks a presiding officer can make to haul him down:

"I'm confused. Will someone summarize what bearing this has on the question before us? . . . We have a decision to make. Is anyone ready to offer a motion? . . . Your point is intriguing, but hadn't we better get back to the motion before us? . . . Can we save your other point until later, and hear from some of the other members on your first point?"

One other fairly common practice wastes a lot of time, although it is meant to save time. This is the technique of the steamroller.

Clarence King, in his *Social Agency Boards*, tells of an agency executive who boasted that he hadn't been voted down by his board in twenty years. Asked how he avoided it, he is quoted: "I sound out a few board members first. They are the three or four who usually decide things. I don't put the matter on the agenda until I know I can win."

Mr. King comments that if "three or four generally decide" then there isn't much use having a board. The other members, jockeyed or steamrollered into agreement with only perfunctory debate, are wasting their time. If they are high-caliber people they know it is wasted, and react accordingly.

The high cost of gloating

Our glossary of time-wasting rites in the board room would be incomplete without a harsh word for reports. Most of them are superfluous gloating.

A board member loves to tell the board about his triumphant fulfillment of a mission. Another member feels obliged to announce that his committee held its regular meeting, and this often draws him into a bit of autobiography or reminiscence. Then the staff wants to "share with" the board some statistics and testimonials. Sometimes whole board meetings are given over to reports, speeches, movies or demonstrations designed to edify and inspire the members.

When such epics are rife, board members silently steal away. The best way to give a board the thrill of accomplishment is to challenge it with tough problems and let it see its progress toward conquering them. (Forgive us for re-emphasizing what we pointed out in the first section of this chapter.)

As for the member who is bursting to report, the president can give him more real satisfaction by receiving his report outside the meeting, if the conversation is well handled. No sane man gets much enjoyment from standing before a big, bored meeting to make a report, especially if his is one of many reports. But telling it to the president face to face can be something a man will enjoy —because of the president's keen attention, pleased expression, warm words, intelligent questions. And, of course, the president's subsequent vivid but fast summary to the board.

How to handle fireworks

"It is frequently the freedom from responsibility that makes persons very ready to say what ought to be done in a very trying situation," pointed out Dr. Thomas F. Kane while president of the University of North Dakota.

"As a man of courage, a president's impulse may be to say 'Damn the torpedoes' and sail straight ahead," added Harold Stoke, president of Queens College. "He may be sure that he will encounter torpedoes, and more likely than not he will get sunk."

Presidents of all sorts may find the above warnings worth noting. Any president is likely to find himself in a controversy now and then.

Of course a smart president tries to anticipate controversy before it comes—not necessarily to dodge it, but to handle it intelligently. One way to cool down hotspurs on the board is to find some way to involve them in responsibility for their rulings. Try to get their advance promise to meet personally with groups they may antagonize. Another way is to keep them informed in advance about any hot questions coming up. Give them as much time as possible to think about it, and as much information as possible, before asking them to take a stand.

Part of a president's duty is to keep his mental sonar plumbing the depths for antagonism. There is always some of it under the surface. In most organizations, writes Paul Pickrel, in *Harper's,* "there is a good deal of free-floating anxiety, generalized dissatisfaction, sense of neglect, and mild paranoia, all of which tend to cluster around the most legitimate cause of discontent available at the moment."

This discontent may be down at the grass roots (see Chapter 9) or in the staff or in the community or on the board itself. It seldom is visible until it erupts. This is why a skilled leader asks open-end questions which don't call for yes or no: questions which begin with "why," or "how should we," or "what reasons do we have for and against," and similar phrases which start people thinking and talking.

At the same time the leader might well be asking a silent question of himself: Am I really interested in what others think, even if it conflicts with my own view? A civic leader should cultivate the art of identifying himself with the end-product of group thinking, rather than with his own contributions or preconceived notions.

People are reluctant to give their true opinions when they lack confidence in each other, according to a study by Glen Mellinger of three hundred members of a large organization. He found that these people could estimate with 91 per cent accuracy the opinions of colleagues whom they trusted, but were wrong 29 per cent of the time in estimating the opinions of those whom they feared or distrusted for any reason.

He also found that communication per se does not increase accuracy in judging another's opinion. When his three hundred people disagreed about an issue, talking it over didn't make them any better able to predict the opinions of those with whom they talked. It sounds incredible, until you realize that much of their disagreement was kept hidden because of lack of confidence.

Therefore a leader who scents opposition to his policies or his organization should take pains to build up confidence between himself and the other parties at issue. His audience's image of him has an important effect on the acceptance of his message.

So it may behoove him to make friends, or to establish his credibility by making verifiable statements, or to demonstrate good intentions by good deeds. When he is talking to those who oppose him (or are likely to oppose him later) he should voice the arguments against him as well as in his favor. This helps to disarm some of the reasoning which skeptics are mentally rehearsing while receiving his message.

Professor James N. Mosel of George Washington University, a wartime specialist in psychological warfare, wrote in *Nation's Business:*

> Your message will be more readily accepted if it is congenial with the attitudes of your audience. If it conflicts, the audience will distort your meaning so as to support, rather than to contradict, their present thinking. If this is not possible, they will reject your message completely. . . . One technique which sometimes helps is for the communicator to state explicitly at the outset that he agrees with the audience. Experimental studies have demonstrated that this method is effective in changing attitudes even when the subsequent part of the message is in disagreement with the audience.

This may sound too cynical for anybody not engaged in psychological warfare, but the underlying implication is perfectly peaceable and valid for all leaders and spokesmen: Search for common ground with your listeners. Shape your message to fit their attitudes. Look at the question from their viewpoint. Map out areas of agreement. You may find that you disagree less than you think.

If there is deep disagreement, a president is ill-advised to trample it down, even when he has a majority. In the words of John L. McCaffrey, president of International Harvester, a president cannot accomplish much without the consent of his constituency, even if he is a Big Boss who can fire people at will. "They must believe in what he is trying to do, if he is to be effective," he writes. "And that is not a matter of giving orders, that is a matter of persuasion, of securing consent."

Many boards try to follow the plan of Quaker meetings, avoiding a vote until the "sense of the meeting" is virtually unanimous. When sides begin to form on some critical question, the chairman calls for more facts to lower the emotional temperature. If necessary he postpones a decision until certain missing information can be obtained. "We've got almost entirely away from voting," one chairman told Stuart Chase. "The facts decide most questions. It makes better feeling in the board, too, for there is no majority to crow and no minority to feel sore."

The importance of buck-passing

The "job specification" for president of any unpaid organization would probably include (1) standing and influence in his community; (2) deep sense of social responsibility; (3) courage and judgment in upholding the principles of his organization; (4) ability to get others to work—which of course means ability to delegate.

The first three relate mostly to the nature of man. The fourth gives the clearest clue to what he is expected to do. He is expected to stimulate other people to work wonders for the group—to "play over their heads," as Henry Kaiser Jr. puts it.

A president can't do this by running most (or even much) of the show himself. There is an old saying in social work that "he who gets ten men to work is better than he who does the work of ten."

An impatient man always finds it easier to do a job himself. But the easiest way isn't necessarily best. A one-man gang as head of a civic organization can wreck it—either by making it so dependent on him that it stops when he steps out, or by alienating other people who could have done work he snatched for himself, or by antagonizing those who disapprove his decisions and/or techniques and/or personality.

Meanwhile, as this dynamo works his head to the bone "for the good of the organization" he is building barriers—because the organization can't operate beyond his personal sphere of action.

Do we hear you asking, "Then what *should* a president do for himself? Surely he shouldn't be a figurehead?"

Your answer, we think, can be found in the "job specification" at the beginning of this section. Let's consider it.

The first requirement for a president—prestige and influence—implies that he should use these assets. He should draw other good men into the movement by inviting them personally. And because of his high standing in the community, a word of thanks from him will mean much more than from anyone who was "delegated" to express appreciation. Here, then, are two duties which a president should keep for himself.

The second specification—sense of social responsibility—implies that the president will pay heed to his organization's impact on other organizations, other interests, other codes. He cannot leave the staff to steer unsupervised. Nor can he shrug his shoulders and murmur, "Whatever the board wants to do is all right with me." He must be a conscience and a lookout for the organization. This responsibility he cannot delegate, though he should share it.

Specification number three—courage and judgment in maintaining standards of his own organization—also implies a job which can't be bucked down to those below him when the heat is on.

Every board, and every staff, is under pressure sometimes to modify its principles or make exceptions. This pressure can come from powerful interests outside, or from people inside, whom the organization can ill afford to lose. The rank and file may join in the pressure, or they may try to hold the line, but if the top man gives way the pressure will be nearly unstoppable. He cannot delegate anyone to fight the big battles for him—although obviously he should enlist allies if he can.

With the above exceptions, an unpaid president ought to delegate virtually everything—including most of the decision-making.

Any student of management is familiar with the second axiom of the American Management Association's code of good organization: *Always give authority with responsibility*. It applies strongly in a volunteer organization. No volunteer worth his salt will take responsibility for a task if he must keep referring to higher authority for decisions.

The risk involved is that his delegate will botch the assignment. If this happens, the president will need the judgment and courage we specified. He must either back up his delegate, making certain he realizes his error and will not repeat it, or must remove him.

In looking at this question of decision-making, don't lose sight of the difference between decisions which an individual must make in implementing an established policy, and those basic decisions as to what the policy should be. It is the difference between the traffic cop and the city council. In volunteer organizations the president should not be the policymaker, nor should any other single person. The president cannot delegate authority to make policy, because this authority is not vested in him. It is vested in the board as a whole.

When a president has inward doubts of the wisdom of a board-made decision, he will nevertheless enforce it loyally—or else resign. However, he seldom faces such a hard choice. Usually he knows more about board business than any other trustee. When he sees a half-baked decision in the making, his remedy is not to flare up with, "If you feel that way about it, I quit," but patiently to help the board learn the facts.

No president should ask his board to follow him blindly. When the board balks, it is usually because trustees know less than he does. In such a predicament he should try to postpone a showdown. Usually his board will agree not to vote until it can get more information. Appointment of a fact-finding committee, or invitation of expert advisers to the next meeting, is a useful avenue to agreement. If this be buck-passing, surely it is better than tricking or pressuring the skeptics. It may take longer. But it builds a wiser, stronger board.

Do we seem to contradict the advice we gave earlier in this chapter against wasting board time in "educating" members? Certainly a board shouldn't whip out decisions without insight. Board members should be well briefed before they act.

A board sometimes deploys most of its membership into a battery of fact-finding committees when it is considering a far-reaching decision. The committees do not report at board meetings. Instead their findings are crystallized in a detailed printed report, which every trustee has leisure to study. Admittedly, this procedure often brings forth a bulky tome—but the tome gets read by the people who helped compile it. If they are the people who base a decision on it, their decision is likely to be wise and virtually unanimous, because they agree on the facts.

Should you hold regular meetings?

"I'm against holding meetings just for the sake of meeting," some presidents growl. "I only call my board together when we have important business to consider."

This is a mad attitude for a board president. (But it is a sane one for a committee chairman, as we saw in Chapter 7. A small working committee should meet when there is work to do, not when the calendar says a fixed interval has elapsed.)

A board of directors, if it is overseeing a staff as most boards do, should meet regularly so the staff can put administrative questions before it. Workers in the field need to ask for board decisions—even if only a decision to approve their own plans.

"Very well, but we still don't need regular board meetings," you may be saying to yourself. "Our board will meet whenever our subordinates have plans ready to be acted upon."

No. Sometimes the agency executive wants to bring up urgent matters of which his board is completely unaware. Furthermore a board usually is too large to be called together on short notice. On the other hand, the staff can usually plan its work so that a short wait for board action won't gum up operations. The regular schedule of board meetings becomes the guide for operations in the field.

Nevertheless, a president is right in insisting that every board meeting should be important. He should keep long-range plans always on the agenda. Projects of the board and its committees should be laid out long in advance, with a timetable for their step-by-step progress. The calendar for a year ahead—five years are better—should be studded with target dates toward which the board is always working.

Under such a plan, why should any board meeting be without an important agenda? If any project, or step in a project, has been completed ahead of schedule, the next item can be moved up. A president who takes the trouble to keep in touch with his subordinates, and inspires them to develop big plans for board consideration, need never have a dull or time-wasting meeting of his board.

Should the professional sit in?

Reverend Roe knows his field—which is preaching and pastoral work—but he would be wasting his time in discussions of finance or of building a bigger plant or of reaching more people. This is the opinion of his church board. Consequently he is not invited to board meetings.

The Young Pirates Association pays a staff to lead youth activities. Therefore the YPA feels its staff should spend their time doing what they're paid for, not sitting through debates on matters of high policy.

The trustees of the Community Chest in New Gehenna, Massachusetts, are sure they know their community, and what it can do, better than any hired fund-raiser. They want no hireling at their meetings telling them what they can or cannot accomplish. They set the goals without advice from him. He runs the campaign the way they tell him to.

The Sacroiliac Society says frankly that its professional director is naturally more interested in piling up an impressive performance record than in trying to meet a great human need. They often remind him of The Limitations of the Expert (to be found in Chapter 9).

Trustees who regularly meet without their expert because of such opinions are sincere but short-sighted. They don't know enough about human nature—or about the efficient organizing of civic causes.

The head of their staff will downgrade them in his own mind. He feels that neither the board nor its executive can do a good job unless there is mutual esteem and clear two-way communication.

Even when the trustees' purpose is simply to conserve their employee's time, he will assume they are discussing secrets they don't want him to hear. He will be sure the board lacks confidence in him.

The president may assure him that everyone is satisfied, but he discounts this. "Why do they meet without me if they think I'm so wonderful?" he asks himself. "Are they planning something I won't like? Obviously they don't want advice from me. To them, I'm just a legman—hired to take orders without back-talk."

Perhaps that is exactly the situation. A board may want only an errand boy and janitor. If so, it can get one for lower salary than it pays a professional social worker.

As mentioned in Chapter 9, and discussed more fully in Chapter 11, experts in community service take pride in their profession. They feel snubbed when not invited to board meetings. Your board may think that nothing which concerns your "hired expert" will be discussed at meetings, and sometimes this may be true— but if you want to show that you respect and trust him, you'll seat him at the board table. You'll ask his opinions. And you'll listen to him.

Even if he is new to his profession, you may be surprised to find that your board's decisions work out better when he helps make them. After all, the man on the ground may see booby-traps which are not noticeable from the heights. In any case, he'll do better work if he understands your point of view.

Besides having the top staff officer present at all meetings, your board may also see the wisdom of inviting other staff members, in regular rotation, to be guests. Of course they shouldn't be expected to say anything unless their chief or the president calls on them. But it's a good idea to be sociable with them, and exchange opinions casually before and after the meeting if not during it. This sort of fraternizing dispels the mystery and aloofness which often isolate a board from its staff.

Evaluation comes but once a year

The previous section was not meant to imply that the professional director should *invariably* be present at board meetings. When his own salary and employment are under discussion, he will not expect—or wish—to be present. Such a discussion can be scheduled for an executive session after the open meeting, or for a special meeting. Either way, the professional should know about it in advance, and know why he is expected to be absent.

Note, however, that the evaluation should be done at annual intervals. To "evaluate" him—pick him to pieces—every month can only breed fear and anger, as anyone with business experience will realize.

In making the actual appraisal, and deciding whether he should be raised or replaced or retained at the same pay, a board might seek answers to such questions as these:

1. Has the work of the organization prospered under his leadership? He really should be the leader in technical matters, not only for the volunteers in the field but also for the board and its presi-

dent. The quality of his leadership (or call it coaching, if you prefer) is measured by the progress of the organization.

2. Does he keep up to date on the state of his art? Since he is a professional he should know the latest advances in his profession, in order to keep the organization from ignorantly making mistakes made elsewhere, and to help it take advantage of new methods.

3. Has he a friendly, approachable, cooperative personality? Does he show poise under stress? Do your volunteers trust him and get inspiriation from contacts with him? Does he win friends for the movement? For himself? Certainly a man who repels people or stirs up opposition is a liability. Granted that he must oppose ideas which he knows to be wrong, he should be tactful.

4. Are his technical skills adequate? Does he plan thoroughly? See his responsibilities clearly? Set objectives? Carry through?

5. Is he reliable in his business management? Does he stay within the budget? Keep accurate records? Analyze facts and figures as a guide in measuring performance and planning ahead?

Perrin Stryker contends in *Fortune* that a really great leader is a rare bird, and that the clearest identification marks are: (a) he has an innate propensity for change and innovation; (b) he manages to change men's beliefs, attitudes and behaviors with benefit to many people.

If your director has these qualities in addition to the formidable list we outlined, probably you had better raise his salary now, before another organization snatches him. When a similar list of criteria for a new president of Yale University was read recently, with the added proviso that he should be a Yale man, someone asked: "But is God a Yale man?"

Danger! Secretary at work

Here is a trick question: Who should take the minutes of the meetings?

To many boards and committees, the answer is deceptively clear: "The professional should take them, perhaps with the help of a stenographer." Sometimes, after the minutes are typed in the agency office, the board secretary glances through them and signs them. In other organizations he doesn't even see them until they are mimeographed and mailed.

Such a system does save bother for the board member who is the titular secretary. But it involves danger.

An agency professional is likely to feel deeply about debates he records. They may effect his career. Is he detached enough to write without shading or omissions? Can he quote everyone correctly?

One board which included district chairmen was planning a fund-raising drive. The minutes reported that "each district chairman accepted responsibility for raising the quota assigned to his district." The fact was that two district chairmen were aghast at their quotas, and had said so. The budget was adopted over their loud protests. When the drive failed and the agency was in the red, these chairmen were blamed for not meeting their quotas after "accepting responsibility" as alleged by the record.

In another case, minutes written by the Pooh-Bah recorded that "it was suggested that the Pooh-Bah try" to keep the expense of a project within certain limits. The trustees thought they had ordered, not suggested, that he stay within the stated limit. But the Pooh-Bah cited the minutes (which had been mailed to every trustee, and routinely approved at board meeting) to justify his overexpenditure.

With the best will in the world, a staff man can honestly misunderstand. Unconsciously he may slant the record just enough to make a vital difference.

The record will shape opinions of absent trustees. It may be exhumed from the files long afterward to shape the opinion of a whole board. Therefore most expert civic workers agree that the staff executive should not write the record of board discussion and action—or that if he does, the elected secretary of the board should check vigilantly for nuances which may be important later.

"But isn't any elected secretary as likely as the professional to make errors?" someone asks.

Of course. The point is that minutes ought always to be triple-checked. No matter who writes them, they should be read by the president, the secretary, and the executive.

Only after all three agree on the record's correctness should it be mimeographed and mailed to the rest of the board. But the writing, agreement, and mailing should all follow promptly after a board meeting, so that every trustee has a chance to catch errors while the meeting is fresh in his mind.

In his *Dynahelps*, Eugene C. Peckham makes another observation worth pondering by all boards. When an elected secretary takes down the minutes himself, he is in a strategic spot to help the board, if he will, in keeping discussion on the track. He can ask questions which seem perfectly natural and unobstructive if he is making the written record:

"Would someone kindly straighten me out?" he may ask. "What are we doing right now which should be put in the minutes?"

Or if someone is talking lengthily but saying little, the secretary may cut in, "Somehow I've lost the trend. Would you give me a brief statement I can jot down?"

When he realizes that members don't see eye to eye, he can ask, "Is everyone clear as to what's going on? What should I record we are agreeing upon at this point?"

Any experienced chairman will recognize how useful such questions can be. Of course the secretary shouldn't try to play Helpful Henry unless he knows the chairman wants him to. And he shouldn't overplay it to the point where it gets irritatingly obvious. But he is the only one who can play it at all. A staff executive who tried it would sound as if he were usurping the chairman's leadership function.

The secretary's work can be more important than it seems. Choose your scribe with care.

CHAPTER 11

Why They Behave Like Social Workers

In any sport, the role of spectator breeds the illusion of personal proficiency.
—JOHN BROOKS

What makes them run

TEN YEARS AGO Mr. Ned Moorefield was in business in Chicago. One day, without a word, his wife took their two babies and vanished. He spent years, and all his savings, trying to locate them, but couldn't get a clue.

Such tragedies are an old story to welfare agencies. Sometimes a social worker writes a happy ending.

It was almost ten years later when, a few days before Christmas, Mr. Moorefield (now in California) got a phone call out of the blue. Mrs. Nita Hansen, of the county welfare bureau in a distant California county, was on the wire. "So we've found you at last!" she said. "Your children are in New Orleans, waiting for you."

Three years earlier his ex-wife had abandoned the children in New Orleans. They were placed in an orphanage, then moved into a foster home. A New Orleans social worker tackled their case. She learned they had an aunt (name unknown) in Hanford,

California. A Hanford social worker located her after six weeks of searching, house to house. The aunt said the children's father was "somewhere in the Los Angeles area." Two social workers in Los Angeles began phoning every Moorefield in every phone book in the vast territory. It took them almost a year, but in the end, the Moorefields got the greatest Christmas present of their lives—from four social workers, laboring for a year for people they didn't know. That's the way social workers are.

They may be caseworkers, group workers, or administrators. They may toil in a church, a school, a hospital or a camp. They vary with the kind of people they try to help, but their differences are less significant than their common denominators. You should understand them, since you'll probably be dealing with them in civic enterprises.

In speaking of the late Reverend Samuel G. Welles of New Jersey, his son once said, "I remember a prominent lawyer to whom my father used to turn when he needed money for some urgent cause. The lawyer told me, 'Your father can get anything he asks because he never asks anything for himself.'

"Just after my father's death a highly cultured and affluent bishop and a poverty-stricken negro ex-convict each told my mother the same thing: 'I have lost my best friend.' Father did try to live up to the best that was in him."

Much the same might be said of many an obscure YMCA secretary, Red Cross chapter worker, Salvation Army lassie, parole officer, Family Service interviewer, Boy Scout field man, and toilers in umpteen other kinds of benevolent calling. They nearly all try, every day of their lives, to live up to the best that is in them.

On the other hand, certain weaknesses are common to many of them—weaknesses of which they are usually aware.

A Tulane professor of social casework, Florence Sytz, has written a widely quoted (within the profession) parody of a welfare conference:

> (1) Profess not to have *the* answer. This lets you out of having any. (2) Say that we must not move too rapidly. This avoids the necessity of getting started. (3) Say that the problem can't be separated from all the other problems. Therefore it can't be solved until all the other problems have been solved. (4) For every proposal set up an opposite one and conclude that the "middle ground" (no motion whatever) represents the wisest course of action. (5) Discover that there are all kinds of "dangers" in any specific formulation or conclusion. (6) Appoint a committee. (7) Wait until an expert has been consulted. (8) State in conclusion that you have all clarified your thinking. This obscures the fact that nothing has been done. (9) Point out that the deepest minds have struggled with the same problem. This implies that it does you credit even to have thought of it. (10) In closing the meeting thank the problem. It has stimulated discussion, opened new vistas, shown us the way, challenged our inventiveness.

So you see social workers can laugh at themselves. And when they roll up their sleeves and wade in to help someone in trouble, the job gets done. But it may take a long time, because after every interview with a troubled person there seemingly must be a long report filed.

"Unlike the other gabby professions, social workers are unchecked by writer's cramps or editorial blue pencils," writes Marion K. Sanders in *Harper's*. "From student days they use dictating machines and are egged on by their supervisors to record a stream-of-consciousness account of the day's doings, known as 'verbatim reporting.'

"At a leading Philadelphia agency 'reporting' is eating up 32 cents of every welfare dollar, according to a recent cost analysis.

"Unfortunately, this verbosity walls off social workers from what they call 'the community,' i.e., non-social workers. Some projects never get off the ground, not because they are foolish, but because the laity finds them dull and obscure."

You need to probe

Probably the last few pages have prepared you for a puzzle in store when you, the plain man, sit across a desk or committee table from paid specialists in benevolent works. You may find them loquacious but immovable if you call for action—or even for a plan of future action—which might lead off the familiar beaten path.

It was Lord Melbourne, the great prime minister of England, who remarked, "Whenever I hear a man say something must be done, I know he's about to do something damn silly." This seems to be an article of faith among many executives of large civic organizations.

True, you mustn't rush into far-reaching commitments. But you may get nowhere at all by forming a committee, or calling a workshop conference, to convene a couple of months from now. You'll have to probe persistently to see whether this conferring is really necessary and what it will accomplish.

You may need to probe even to understand the odd dialect spoken by most social workers. As Marion Sanders points out, they never tell you anything; instead they "share information" with you. If anything is poorly planned it is "unstructured." Helping somebody get a job is "environmental manipulation." Instead of publicity, selling an idea takes "interpretation." The worker in a welfare office "functions in an agency setting." She doesn't care whether you like her but hopes you will "relate positively" to her.

"What does this mean in simple language?" is a question you may need to ask often. "Why is this so? Please give me some examples."

Group work professionals are likely to be more crisp, energetic and perhaps even domineering than their colleagues in casework. They are planners, go-getters, do-it-now types. A group worker may have a mania for enrolling bigger and bigger groups, and more and more of them, as fast as possible. He may want larger camps, larger buildings, larger paid staffs, larger budgets. If you probe, you may find that he is under pressure from higher-ups in his profession or his board.

One clergyman wrote: "Ministers are used to threatening letters from their hierarchy. Bishops and superintendents frequently remind them: 'We are taking careful note'—whether or not you are meeting your quota, whether or not you support this or that program. 'A record will be kept.'"

Perhaps this is part of our American passion for statistics. We like to be record-breakers. "Bigger" is almost a synonym for "better" in our lexicon.

It's only when we stand off for a cool look at the larger perspective that we see where we're headed. That's why broad-gauged board members are needed, to balance the experts and apply the brakes occasionally.

Because social work votaries now enter their profession young, they lack knowledge of the varied world outside it. Social work is a career. Young people enter it with degrees and diplomas from schools which teach special doctrines and expertise.

This is as it should be. A board which employs a professional wants a skilled one. But it should look out for his occupational weaknesses. It should nourish, protect, and nudge him.

They need to squirm

Complacency is a malady to which we all are prey. Your agency professionals may need inoculating against it at intervals, with a gentle but well-aimed needle.

The rector of one big church in Angelton inaugurated a monthly Fellowship Supper, and thought it a great success. He squirmed when an analytical vestryman counted heads and pointed out that only 27 per cent of the people invited had come. "I dare say other churches in Angelton get a much lower percentage," the rector barked.

He bridled when the vestryman checked and found this wasn't so. Then the vestryman proposed canvassing absentees to learn why they hadn't come. Irritably, the rector agreed.

He was a powerful preacher. His church was jammed at all services. But the canvass showed that the bulk of his congregations weren't church members; they were outsiders attracted by pulpit showmanship. Crowded out, members of the church felt unwelcome.

When he understood what was happening, the rector remedied it with personal calls on disaffected members. Much bigger fellowship suppers, as well as bigger enrollments in Sunday School and other church activities, were the result.

E. St. Elmo Lewis, speaking as an advertising man to a national conference of social work executives, told them, "When you are selling your program to a businessman he'll ask first, What is it? Then, How does it work? Then, What will it accomplish? And finally—*How do you know?*"

"How do you know?" should evoke data on which tough-minded judges, not emotionally involved, can evaluate a civic undertaking. Social work would be more fruitful if this question were asked oftener. We need more measurement of the effectiveness of our programs—and we need businessmen to do this measuring.

Rewards of the inquisition

In a factory district of Los Angeles, hundreds of boys who

needed Scouting badly are now getting it—because one factory manager kept asking questions and pushing for businesslike methods.

The district swarmed with boys. But this was a low-rent, low-income area. People who lived there wanted their boys to be Scouts, but they knew nothing of organization or administration. So the program languished. Scout membership shrank each year.

Mr. Robert W. Maney didn't live in the area but he worked there, as manager of the Goodyear plant. When asked to become chairman of the Scout district committee, he agreed.

At his first session with Vern Dunn, the Scout professional in that district, Maney's first question was naturally, "What am I expected to do?"

"Build an organization of volunteers which will bring Scouting to more boys," Dunn told him, and listed the volunteer committees which function in a Scout district.

"Now let me have copies of the job descriptions for each of these committees," Maney said.

Dunn was stumped, because the outline in the bylaws wasn't explicit. However, he was a seasoned field worker, and with some head-scratching he put together a precise itemization of what each committee should do.

"Now I want to meet with each of these committee," Maney told him. "Will you arrange a series of noon meetings?"

The executive was dismayed. "These men are factory workers. They can't get away for lunch."

"Then we'll get men who can. This job can't be done by men who can't command their own time." Taking the executive with him, he went calling on merchants and management men of the kind he needed—people who worked in the area but lived elsewhere.

As each man accepted, he was given a clear briefing of his mission. "Let's set objectives, and keep track of progress toward them," Maney said. "We'll want to agree on deadlines. In reporting to me, just fill me in on your progress—not your difficulties. Discuss the difficulties with Vern Dunn, here, and he'll help you solve them."

Vern Dunn had never been so hustled in his life. Maney would accept no half-answers either from him or a committee chairman. "If you don't know, please say so, and then find out—fully," he kept insisting.

In the three years he was chairman of the district, its Scout membership rose 26 per cent while other districts made normal gains of about 4 per cent a year. "It was the hardest work I ever did," Dunn said, "but I sure learned a lot."

Good meddling and bad

There is a twilight zone in many organizations, where the powers of the board and the executive overlap.

Should the executive be free to choose his own assistants, or has the board the right to pass on them? Should the board gossip with assistants behind the director's back? Who can fire the assistants? Who should fix their salaries?

These are delicate questions. A wrong answer can wreck an organization. The Pro Bono Public League in Chaos Falls appointed a new executive secretary, who found on arrival that he had inherited a nice old man as assistant, a former board member who had been hired out of pity when retired from his former employment. Beloved by all, he was totally ineffective, but the board wouldn't consider releasing him. So the executive was handcuffed.

The president of another agency in New Gehenna told the staff, "Come to me if you have any friction with the new chief." He was trying to be helpful. Actually, he was undermining the chief, of course.

It's common sense to put the hiring, firing, and supervision in the hands of the executive. But some safeguards may be needed. Many trustees are versed in arts of personnel selection and evaluation which their director knows little about.

A sound plan might be to appoint a committee of trustees with personnel-work experience to write a job description of any staff position which is to be filled. They should consult with the executive, of course. But they should hold out for veto power over any candidate he suggests.

But they'd better not force the executive to hire (or keep) anybody he doesn't want. If they do this, they might as well replace the executive. He'll be little use to them thereafter.

As a board member, you can do a couple of things which may seem none of your business, but actually will help. One is to recognize that staff people get discouraged.

Seeing his work as important enough to call him to a lifetime of service, the professional sets his goals so high that he often falls short. Moreover, there are plenty of critics around to reiterate what he's telling himself: that he isn't much good. Most professionals learn to live with this and rise above it, but they'll be more buoyant if they hear a kind word occasionally from you and your ilk.

Another bit of benign meddling you might perform is to drag your director into some activities totally unrelated to his work. The job can easily become a seven-day round-the-clock occupation, and professionals tend to make it their whole life. On the day when they leave the office for the last time, minus their "contact file," they find themselves alone and friendless. If you like your director, get him to widen his world. Some day he'll be glad you did.

Do you demand too much?

In the city of Euphoria, the trustees of the Mental Health Foundation hired a professional executive after they had tried and failed to raise funds without one. Someone told them that a good executive could readily bring in many times as much money as was paid. So they hired a whirlwind from Chaos Falls, promising him $10,000 a year, and sat back to watch the big gifts roll in.

Of course it didn't work. Any board which expects a new executive, on his own, to scrape acquaintance with the city's moneyed men and coax them to bestow large sums is naïve. The board must introduce him to the right people and help him cultivate them.

Laymen also may expect too much of their paid staff in other ways. They may expect a minister to organize and supervise all the church suppers, bazaars, Sunday School classes, choir practices, and other activities of the pastorate. They may think the YMCA secretary should keep the building painted and serve as lifeguard at the pool.

Most community agencies depend on laymen, and plenty of them, to get the work done. A Scout troop needs an active troop committee behind it. The complex operation of a church calls for dozens of planners and doers. And in agencies serving the whole city, or the nation, the work performed by volunteers wouldn't get done if left to paid staffs.

So if there's more work to be done than your professional can handle, don't blame him. Pitch in and help—even if yours is one of the few organizations where the professional is reluctant to let the laity into the act. The very fact that high-powered men and women are willing to work without pay is what makes community service effective.

—or too little?

On the other hand, most agencies would shake themselves to pieces or rust away if they didn't have some dedicated experts who spent full time keeping the wheels oiled.

Almost without exception, agencies which try to conduct finance campaigns without professional help raise less money (and spend a higher percentage for expenses) than those which employ a real pro.

Likewise, when one agency in Chaos Falls made laymen operate the whole program for six weeks while its staff spent full time on a membership drive, they couldn't hold the members brought in by the staff. And when the Friendly Cannibals closed down the New Gehenna office for the summer while the staff went off to run the camp, it lost so many volunteers and members that reconstruction took two years.

The question isn't how much, or how little, work to expect from your staff. The confusion is in *what kind* of work to expect from them. How to divide the burden between laymen and staff?

This question wouldn't puzzle an amateur theatrical group. If they hire a director they don't expect him to play the roles, build scenery, or sell tickets. They know he is hired to coach. He helps them improve their technique, but they run the show.

The same principle applies to almost any civic work done by nonprofessionals with a paid executive. They should think of him as their coach. A good rule of thumb, as stated by one executive, is, "I do only the things which nobody else can do."

Training in method is of course his special function. He may also be expected to make a lot of speeches, especially to audiences which want technical or historical detail. And he should furnish accurate information about the organization's progress (or retrogression). This calls for records and clerical work which volunteers seldom handle well. Paid office help is usually good economy. Why require your director to do a clerk's work if you pay him an expert's salary?

You should expect wise and knowing advice from him, as you do from your lawyer. At the same time, when he urges some policy upon you, your duty is to make sure he isn't riding some hobbyhorse of his own. You always have—and should exercise—the right to ask him, "How do you know?"

CHAPTER 12

Off with His Head

When to fire the executive

FROM BOTH SIDES of the board-executive fence, people should reach across with trusting smiles. The amateurs and the pro ought to pull together as equals, and friends.

But the time may come when mutual trust and esteem die. Then the executive should go.

If you serve on several boards, eventually the law of averages is likely to catch you in the old, painful controversy: to fire or not to fire the executive?

The answer may be clear, if he's manifestly incompetent. But he may be highly competent and yet in the shadow of the ax, for reasons good or bad.

Let's consider first the kinds of predicament which should compel the exit of a competent managing director.

1. When the board feels it must overrule him after he has discharged a subordinate. If overruled in such a struggle, the chief loses all power over the subordinate.

While good administration requires that the executive ask his board's approval in passing the pink slip, the board must recognize it is making a fateful choice: it must either approve the discharge or get a new managing director.

2. When the executive gets too proprietary—e.g. insists that

the organization must be run as he sees fit. Sometimes a board finds itself overseeing a director who thinks of his smallest decrees as Divine Revelation. Even if prudent enough not to act without board approval, he may be so touchy about prerogatives that he flares up at a hint of criticism.

However, before condemning him, a board should give long thought to the situation. This man may have built the organization from nothing. Perhaps his sweat and tears have gone into it for years, while board members painlessly came and went. How can he help feeling that he is Mr. Organization?

Yet when he is basically at odds with his constituency he must be shown as tactfully as possible that the organization belongs not to him but to the members and public (as represented by the board). If his board feels dependent on him, and knuckles under repeatedly to his open or implied ultimatum of *Do as I say or get another executive,* then why have a board?

A too-powerful or too-proud executive ought to be removed, not only because he is making dummies of his trustees, but because he lacks judgment. He should know that his organization's success in the long run requires a thinking, functioning board.

3. When a strongly entrenched trustee is at war with the executive. This assumes, of course, that the rest of the board is unwilling or unable to get rid of the belligerent trustee. There's no use hoping the board can simply keep voting him down. An implacable critic on a board will sooner or later pull the best executive off his perch, and meanwhile there'll be continuous harm to the organization.

There was a widely known case of this kind some years ago in San Diablo, Texas. A high-powered, hard-driving industrialist joined the board of the Community Chest, which had a fine executive. The newcomer, at his first board meeting, banged the table and yelled for a drastic change in agency policy. No trustee had the mettle to argue with him, so the executive felt duty-bound to point out the dangers of such a change. While the thwarted tycoon turned turkey red, his proposal was voted down. Afterwards he privately told the executive, "I'm going to get your job."

He did. It took two years but it was inevitable. He made every meeting too hot for comfort. Some trustees resigned. Those who remained finally quenched the flame by discharging the director.

The agency may or may not have suffered by substituting a more pliant executive. The point is that two years was too long for both men to be connected with the same agency.

4. When the executive's private life puts him deeply at odds with the organization or the public.

Occasionally some board finds that its talented executive is running heavily into debt; or his wife is leaving him; or his son is in trouble. Or he may have habits which the community finds unacceptable—drinking, smoking, or (in one actual case) going to movies on Sunday.

Must the trustees dismiss him? If he is capable, of course they should first try to help him. A banker on the board may show him how to make his peace with creditors. Other board members may give him sympathetic counsel to ease other kinds of trouble.

But if the trouble persists, trustees must be realistic, must put the organization's best interests ahead of the director's. Reasonably or not, he is seen as a walking advertisement for the organization. If he gives many people a bad opinion of it, to that extent he is bad for it.

Whom are you high-hatting?

On the other hand, there are times when a board should stand firm against demands for its executive's scalp.

Such demands come most commonly from within the board itself. They are likely to arise if trustees look on their executive as a barely tolerable necessity, like the golf pro in a 1910 country club.

Differences of opinion, big or little, between executive and trustees can lead to animosity when a trustee takes the attitude that "This guy seems to forget he's on salary, and we pay it." If such a spirit exists anywhere on your board, some soul-searching may be in order. Just how is a full-time paid social worker inferior to a board member? Why should he look up to you?

The director you employ is seldom as well stocked with worldly goods as his board members. But he feels himself their compeer in other ways. The lower income is his by choice. He might earn more in other fields.

His situation differs from that of the general manager of a business. He sees himself as a public servant; not as your personal servant; not even as your employee. His role, in his own eyes and in actual fact, is like that of your doctor or lawyer. He respects the trustees' proficiency in their professions, but he wants similar respect in his.

If they patronize him, bawl him out, or make him their errand boy, he'll resent it. He has a right to. For fundamentally he is a full partner in your enterprise, brought in to give expert advice and technical assistance. Of course his advice won't always be taken. But if trustees think they're too big to listen to his advice—in the realm where he's the expert—he can't do his job.

Enemies at the gates

Although cool heads and warm hearts are enough to keep the peace between an executive and his board, there will be times when wolves howl, outside the board room. And sometimes a board is tempted to throw the executive to the wolves—or sit quietly while the wolves come for him.

In any kind of civic work, a paid professional is the symbol of his organization, and therefore is the target of the public's wrath whenever anything goes wrong. At such times he needs protection by his board—needs it desperately.

Isn't this true in your town? The clergyman is thought of as the spokesman for his church. The Community Chest secretary is the one who answers the phone, does the explaining. The superintendent of schools "bosses" the school system, or so it seems to teachers and parents. Seldom do critics remember that these administrators are governed by boards.

The smart executive, when pressed to grant some favor against regulations, tries to avoid giving a ruling. "I see your point," he says, "and I'll see if the board is willing to make an exception in your case." Then he lets the board president write a letter explaining the rule and why it cannot be broken.

This isn't cowardly buck-passing. It is prudent public relations, for the good of your organization. The value of your executive is lessened if the public thinks him unfriendly or uncooperative. In other words, the trustees must step forth and take responsibility for unpopular decisions.

Whenever a board hears sniping against its executive from any significant source, trustees should go out of their way to defend him staunchly. If he's in the wrong, perhaps that's another story. The board may want to defend him anyhow in public, and correct him in private, or it may choose to repudiate him—which usually necessitates replacing him. But when he's fighting the good fight for established policies, the board must back him vigorously or his value is destroyed.

Iago in the woodpile

PLEASE PLAN TO ARRIVE EVENING MARCH 7, the president of a family service agency wired its newly hired executive. AM GIVING DINNER TO INTRODUCE YOU TO THE BOARD.

The new man—let's call him Mike Morpheus—was conscientious

about tying up loose ends in his previous position. So he didn't get away until the night of the sixth. He drove all night and all next day, arriving just in time for the dinner at the president's home. After dinner the board sat around a roaring grate fire while each member talked at length. Then the president made a sonorous speech introducing the new executive.

When he turned to Mike, awaiting his response, the luckless executive was sound asleep.

Mike apologized as best he could, but the furious board had mentally condemned him already. They dropped him at the end of the year.

Mike went on to a brilliant career in another organization. We tell the story here to illustrate how capriciously a board can turn against its executive.

Sometimes a board member's cold drive for power is behind an attack on an executive. It happened that way in the Community Chest office of a city we'll call Bigburg.

The Chest in the nearby suburb of Sunken Heights couldn't finance itself, so it asked to be annexed to the Bigburg association. This was done. The Sunken Heights professional, John Silver, came on the Bigburg staff. He soon began boring from within to get the top job.

Gus Caesar, the Bigburg skipper, had held his job for twenty years. His board thought highly of him. Nevertheless, rumors started that Gus might retire and that John was in line to replace him. Gus kept denying the rumors.

Then scandal started. Gus (a married man) was being "seen around town" with the switchboard girl (also married) from the Chest office.

This was true, in a way. Gus lived twenty miles from the Chest office, and the girl's apartment was on his route home. Sometimes he held staff conferences in the office until six o'clock, and the girl stayed on to handle their phone calls. When this happened,

Gus usually offered her a ride home, to save her a long wait for a bus.

But these details were never included in the vague reports which kept tongues wagging. On the board a body of quiet opinion developed that Gus should be forced to take early retirement. (Look back to the Rule of Three, in Chapter 3.)

But Gus was a fighter. He made the president call a special meeting of the board. There he brought the issue into the open, demanding that the board investigate. The old man was so belligerent, and so beloved by trustees who had worked with him for years, that they rallied to him. They forced John Silver to apply for transfer to a Chest office in another state.

If you're a board member, when daggers come out at the board table look for hidden motives. Look for old grudges. Don't be quick to judge by appearances or hearsay.

Will he starve if you fire him?

More than a few career men in social-service work have dropped into limbo after losing executive jobs. Some became cab drivers or night watchmen. Some died as paupers or took their own lives.

Such cases are rarer than they used to be. Today pension plans, health insurance, nationwide placement service and other safeguards for professionals are built into many national welfare organizations. But the penalties of getting fired may be severe even now.

The possible penalties are loss of income, loss of self-confidence, and damage to reputation. The second and third may fatally impair a man's ability to get any important job in his own field.

Loss of income is a sharper blow to a social work executive than to the average businessman. Salary scales are still low in the welfare world. The chances of accumulating a cushion against unemployment are slim.

In this field, as in business, a summary firing may wreak deep psychological damage. "Men who are injured this way seem to be bleeding internally," says one placement director. "They aren't themselves for years afterward."

Moreover, the grapevine in each field of social work is pervasive. If the top executive is thrown out of an adoption agency in Seattle or a home for the blind in Denver, adoption workers or blind workers all over the country will hear of it. The jobless executive may find himself marked as a failure throughout his own profession.

A few movements have national and regional personnel departments. These organizations can often find other berths for their jobless executives—sometimes without his even knowing that his board instigated the transfer. If the personnel bureau judges him unfitted for a post of the magnitude he lost, it may conclude that he'll shine in a smaller one, and seek out a snug berth for him.

But this is not inevitable. Sometimes a board ejects its executive suddenly and theatrically, so that a transfer becomes difficult.

If a social work executive has no placement bureau to help him, his problem is more dire—and the board's moral duty to temper justice with mercy is correspondingly imperative. Aren't there gentle ways to ease him out?

Certainly he can be allowed to save face by resigning. And perhaps he can be given several months to look around before quitting.

Another humane course is to help him find a connection outside the organization. There are influential people on the board who can open doors for him.

The heat of a board meeting hell-bent on busting somebody is a difficult climate in which to argue for clemency. But the argument should be made. As one trustee said in resisting clamor to dismiss an executive on the spot, "Much as we dislike this man, we'll sleep better at night if we send him out with a good prospect ahead of him. Let's make sure we don't ruin him when we fire him."

You too can throw boomerangs

A youth organization in the city of New Gehenna fired a manager who had spent thirty years building the organization there. He hadn't done anything culpable, but he was getting deaf. When his handicap became obvious, the board abruptly dropped him.

He was fifty-five. He was supporting his mother, his wife and three children. The board didn't discuss his future prospects. "We can't be sentimental about this," said some of the practical trustees. "The old fellow isn't cutting the mustard. We owe it to the youth of New Gehenna to replace him."

The discharged executive sank his scanty savings in opening a machine shop. In a few months he moved to the shabbiest part of town. Within a year he died.

When it reached the ears of the thousands of graduates and supporters of the movement, their wrath shook the city. Every member of the unsentimental board of trustees was hit where he felt it most. One trustee, a newspaper publisher, lost advertising and subscriptions. Another, a merchant, lost customers and suppliers. An aircraft executive was ostracized by other people in his company and eventually had to resign.

Meanwhile the board found it couldn't hire any new staff people. The movement's professionals all over the country had heard the story and decided that the New Gehenna board would be a dangerous employer.

Volunteer workers resigned in droves. Parents yanked their

children out. Fund-bestowers shut purses. Seeing all this erosion, the Community Chest tightened the agency's budget. It took ten years for the agency to recover from a decision made in half an hour by its trustees.

Similar true stories could be told in many communities. If your board is lining up a firing squad, beware of backfires. The most incompetent executive has friends, and is bound to tell them his side of the story. They will spread and embellish it. May it not be better to avoid all this by finding some kindly way to put the executive out to pasture?

CHAPTER **13**

We've Lost Our Executive

The perils of promoting from within

A CRISIS confronted the directors of the Myopia League in the city of Macropolis. The executive was retiring. The board had to find a new professional to replace him.

Mr. Ranx, the president, drew on his business lore and proposed a quick solution: "Move up one of the assistants. That's what we do in my corporation. When the president dies we hire a new office boy."

Other trustees nodded. "Much better for morale. If staff know they have a chance to climb to the top job, they'll work harder and stay with us longer."

"Besides, a local staffer knows the local situation," another said.

So the board agreed to promote one of the assistants. But which one? Each staffer discreetly lined up partisans. Blocs formed. After a free-for-all in board meeting, the job went to Bill Bragg, an assistant executive who mustered the loudest-talking and most powerful friends.

Soon other staff people, seeing that their board had encouraged them to climb, got busy with poison and soft soap. Whenever one happened to be chatting with some board dignitary who wondered why Chief Bragg did things a certain way, an assistant might give the chief a boost between the shoulder-blades. "Dear old Bill! A grand guy in his way. We know the years he's spent in this work, but—"

Each staff man diligently registered charm and oomph among his coterie of board people. Instead of reporting to Chief Bragg, and seeking assignments from him, the assistants thought first about impressing trustees. Everybody spread word about mishaps of other assistants and the chief. Everybody solicited suggestions from trustees, and obeyed with the flourish of an Oriental djinn.

The chief didn't know why he was by-passed so often, or why his staff people suddenly distrusted each other. He was busy try-ing to learn his own job. He'd discovered that it called for an arsenal of skills an assistant couldn't learn: administering a big staff, finding and shepherding high-level volunteers, unfolding the mysteries of the movement to consequential outsiders, master-minding the all-important fund-raising.

But President Ranx thought everything was splendid. He could see the staff were on their toes, more than ever before. They were friendlier, too. Told him more. Scrambled to do thoughtful little favors for board people. Fine spirit!

At a national meeting of the Myopia Leagues of America, Ranx made a powerful speech urging promotion-from-within as a mandatory policy throughout the movement. "It would be an inspiration to the whole chain of command," he said. "No longer would assistants see a man from another Myopia office brought in over their heads."

To trustees with business or military backgrounds, Ranx sounded eminently sensible. His motion carried by acclamation.

From then on, Myopia League career men jockeyed and jostled to get onto staffs of big-city Myopia offices. Each staff was walled in because of the new policy; nobody could transfer from city to city except at the lowest levels. Those who failed to find a metropolitan foothold soon turned away from the movement and sought some other lifework. Why take a Myopia job in a smaller city? Once there, they'd have no route to the top.

Thus enfeebled by hardening arteries and thinning blood, the movement declined. Today Myopia in America seems doomed.

There are still a few national movements like this. Intrigue and push, though not downright defamation, play a part in self-advancement. A former clergyman recently wrote of his church in *Harper's* magazine: "Probably the most serious charge which the young minister would make is that he is forced into playing the role of a politician if he is to get ahead. . . . The outright bootlicking, backslapping, and apple-polishing which go on in the aggressive fight for position, place, and prestige are appalling to any sensitive young minister. The leading laymen expect it and foster it."

However, the great majority of churches and other national movements take the opposite tack: town-to-town promotion by local boards, with an iron rule that no assistant can step up to replace his own chief. Consider the advantages:

1) The ambitious staffer then knows his advancement depends on pleasing not the board but the executive. He has an incentive to prove himself a good team worker, worth recommending for a vacancy elsewhere.

2) Small communities aren't harmed, even though their executives come and go, using them as stepping stones. A small town gets a continuing supply of new brooms, sweeping vigorously to win renown so they'll qualify for bigger jobs.

3) When a top vacancy opens, everybody understands that an outsider *must* be brought in; the board can calmly appraise candidates on their records.

4) A new executive (except in the small one-man offices) has already mastered the special skills needed for the top spot. He learned them as top man in a smaller town.

A new social worker, just plunging into the profession, usually lands on a big-city staff. (This isn't always so, but metropolitan

offices have more openings and hire more rookies.) He's likely
to be teamed with an older hand who'll supervise him closely.

After a few years he may be called to join the staff of a smaller
office where he'll be one of a handful, working directly under the
executive's eye. Here he'll be more of an all-round utility man.

Next he's in line for executiveship, but in a one-man agency.
Now he'll carry all the bundles—program, recruiting, training,
public relations, finance. But if he fumbles a few, the harm isn't
great. Board members can back him up where he's weak. And
once he's a seasoned virtuoso, the top jobs in bigger cities beckon.
At every rung he can rise without knifing anyone, and his employers can get the best that's in him.

The only hazard in this system is the chance that an executive
may be tempted to cling to a high-powered assistant rather than
recommend him for promotion elsewhere. However, any chief
who didn't cooperate with Personnel would get precious few
good names from Personnel when *he* needed staff.

Seek and ye shall find

So you're looking for a new executive.

He may not be in sight at the moment. But finding him isn't
as hard as it sounds. Is your local group part of a national movement? Then it has a national personnel bureau—perhaps even a
regional one—which can recommend candidates and give you their
dossiers.

Or is your group strictly local, with no state or national affilia-
tions? Then try the social work magazines. They print news and
advertisements about available vacancies and available people.
Other movements similar to yours will have executives who want
to make a change.

"If he wants to change, he must be in trouble where he is,"
some people assume, especially if the candidate holds a job about

the same size as the one they're seeking to fill.

But this isn't necessarily true. Where he is now, your prospective executive may be bumping against a salary ceiling. Or he may need to move because of the health of someone in his family. Or he may be rubbed raw by a personality clash which isn't his fault. Sometimes, too, a fine social worker feels he's solved all the major problems where he is, and yearns like Alexander for new worlds to conquer, even at lower pay if need be.

What if an executive has just been ousted from his job? As shown in the previous chapter, people in community service often get fired unfairly. One of them may be valuable to you for the very reason that got him fired: refusal to play politics or go along with good-enough-for-Grandpa thinking.

So spread news of your vacancy. Put out feelers among volunteers and professionals in your own and similar movements. You may be amazed at the number of good possibilities who pop up.

Take time to study as many candidates as you can. In the meantime the local staff of assistants can probably keep things running smoothly for months, if they must. Even if yours is a one-man agency, and you have to rely entirely on volunteers in the interim, isn't this better than buying a lemon for your agency?

How to investigate a candidate

As a prudent businessman, you needn't be reminded that the first rule in picking an employee from a pack of candidates is to investigate. But your investigative process is a bit different here, isn't it, than in the business market place?

The man you're picking now will need to be, in the words of Casey Stengel, "a man of many facets, all turned on." Your man will deal with more sorts and conditions of people than a business employee would. He'll need cooperation from churchmen, union kingpins, police chiefs, newspaper editors, club presidents. He'll work with conglomerate hierarchies of racial minorities, political parties, civic groups, financial and industrial fraternities.

As for references, every candidate names his pals and boosters, quite automatically. If you write to them, you'll get eulogies. Why not phone them instead? You'll doubtless get eulogies anyhow, but you can ask a few searching questions: "What organizations has he worked with? Where else has he lived and worked? What clubs has he joined and later left?"

Of course this doesn't mean you're on a muckraking expedition. All you want is an accurate picture of the candidate's history and personality—his human failings as well as his virtues. You'll never get this by collecting To Whom It May Concern letters from his best friends.

Dig for facts and figures about a candidate's past performance. Compare them with the record of his predecessors or other people in similar spots. The surface data you get from the personnel bureau, or from the applicant, won't tell the whole story.

Why does he want to move? He'll state plausible reasons. But are there other reasons too? Are there reasons he himself doesn't recognize?

Probably you realize, now, that some board member ought to visit each candidate's city before the board chooses between the two or three finalists. People will divulge information in a face-to-face chat which they'd hesitate to put in a letter or tell a stranger on the phone.

Your investigator on the spot can judge the consensus of the whole community. If nobody on your board can go there, perhaps a board member knows some business associate living there who will investigate for you.

While investigating, you'll naturally need a fairly exact vision of what manner of man you want. Attempts are often made to draw up a "job specification" for a social work executive. However, Clarence King has this to say in his *Social Agency Boards:*

The wise choice of a qualified executive is probably the most difficult task any board can face. The qualities which should be possessed by the ideal executive, if he is to be a wise leader of both his staff and his board, are so varied that seldom will they all be found in one human being. A committee of social work executives attempted to list the qualities which any executive should possess. After weeks of deliberation the incompleted list stood at 18.

They finally abandoned their attempt as absurd, one of them declaring that they were trying to write the specifications for an archangel.

Where does this leave us? If we can't write a job description, how can we pick a man for it?

Professor King goes on to suggest two possible methods used by many boards. Although they can't find an archangel they can at least decide which of his many traits are most necessary. Having found a few men with the absolute essentials, they can then look to see who comes nearest to meeting their other standards.

The second method—often used in combination with the first— is to consider the vacancy in the framework of the whole staff. Whichever qualities the top man lacks should be supplied by his lieutenants, or possibly by prominent figures on his board. Therefore you may want to look over the present personnel, and perhaps add to it, when bringing in a new executive.

Interviewing candidates is pointless until you've narrowed the field to a few. However, after evaluating and investigating, the board or a committee will doubtless need to summon the prospective new executive to be decorously grilled, like a frankfurter at the Waldorf.

Some boards put the finalist candidates through a pressure interview, as personnel experts call it. Questions come smoking in like tracer bullets. The candidate may hear himself politely (or even violently) contradicted and ridiculed. Why not? He'll surely get savaged now and then in almost any kind of civic work. This may be a good time to see how he keeps his poise. Afterward, of course, he'll be congratulated and assured that the only purpose of the rough handling was to let him prove he could take it. But there's a danger here, as we'll see in the next section.

He may not want the job

A pressure interview can blow up in a board's face. Many gifted executives won't tolerate it. They'll walk out.

Any experienced managing director knows he'll sometimes be faced with uproar and protest. He may be willing and able to handle them diplomatically when there's an important principle at stake—yet be quite unwilling to work under trustees resembling peevish tribal gods who say it with thunderbolts. While the board is sizing him up, he's doing likewise to the board.

A qualified candidate for director of an agency seldom comes hat in hand. Around the nation there usually are more vacancies than executives. Many a board screens a set of applicants, picks the man it wants, proffers him a sizable raise over his current income, then hears him say, "Thanks, but I've decided I wouldn't fit." This often happens even if there has been nothing resembling a pressure interview.

Good social workers will accept a niche only if they're sure it's an opportunity for worth-while service, with sympathetic allies on the board and elsewhere. A visit to a strange city may repel them. They may conclude it's an undesirable place to live and bring up children, or to work—at least for anyone of their calling and income. Maybe they hear that the agency is known for arrogance, or for penny-pinching in travel allowances and vacations, or for quarrelsome factions. You'd be surprised how much is said about your board in the agency down the block or the city across the river.

You face the same problem as a trapper from the aviary. After a search to find the proper bird, you must emit dulcet wooing sounds. Stated less fancifully, a selling job confronts you. You must convince your prospect that he wants to work in your agency.

If you've had undue turnover among executives, it might pay to find out why—and do something about it, and tell your prospect.

Let the man know why you want him above anyone else, and what you think he can do. Lay the agency's difficulties before him frankly. Indeed, they may be your juiciest bait. He'll smack his lips if he can envision himself breaking new ground, working for people who need him and value him and like him.

Tell him frankly why your former managing director left. If it was for a bigger job elsewhere, that's fine. It labels your job as a promising springboard. If he left—or was pushed—because of trouble, the whole tale should be told the prospective replacement. Sooner or later he'll hear it from other sources. Every alert candidate studies your terrain like an Indian scout for traces of hostiles before he moves in. Let him feel sure that no ambushes await him. He won't fear a few enemies if he knows where they are.

All that remains is to agree on a salary which gives his family a decent standard of living, and which lets him feel he's bettering himself by moving. Basically he wants an opportunity for significant service in a congenial setting. If you can offer him this, truthfully and convincingly, he'll come.

Don't forget the launching

So you've signed him up. Now will you leave him alone to make his own way? Not if you want him to succeed.

Before he arrives, his path should be paved with press releases and announcements to the agency membership. His picture should be in the newspapers. If he creeps into town unheralded, how long will it take him single-handed to establish the prestige and connections your board could hook up for him almost instantly?

Shouldn't you plan receptions where he'll meet key people? Shouldn't you arrange speaking engagements for him, so he'll quickly become known as spokesman for your agency? How about introducing his wife into a circle of friends? How about inviting him to club meetings and social festivities?

"Been-here don't go with come-here," as a proud lady in a Southern village once expressed it. Thousands of years earlier Xenophon put it more drastically: "Because you come from across the river we must kill you. If you came from our side of the river we would not have to kill you." People are more mobile and receptive now, but they still feel instinctively cool to a stranger who comes to take charge of an organization they regard as their own. You can break down much of that reserve, if you will.

You can be especially useful in propitiating potential troublemakers. You know who they are. The new man doesn't. Why not take him around and introduce him? Very likely he can hitch them into his team, if they're not left to watch suspiciously from afar. Public relations experts have an axiom, "The better people know you, the more willing they are to do business with you." And they also advise, "Make your friends before you need them."

Overtures to your new man's potential allies around town should be made at once: the heads of other local organizations, the city fathers and other movers and shakers. This is especially important if your agency's relations with them weren't altogether neighborly under the old regime; this is your chance for a rapprochement. Small informal lunches with the foreign powers are logical and timely at this point; if neglected now, they'll come harder later.

In addition to this public launching, much can be done to help your new executive get settled privately. He'll be house-hunting;

board members can advise him as to good neighborhoods, and even hunt up desirable homes within his means. Bank credit may be important to him also. One new executive was invited by a banker on his board to borrow $500 for six months. The executive saw no reason to go into debt—until the banker explained how useful the bank's credit reference could be in buying a house, a car, home furnishings or other necessities.

Thoughtful steps such as these, with similar gestures to help his wife and children feel welcome, will accomplish more than you may realize. In addition to making your director happier and more effective, they'll be noised around in professional circles. Later on, when your agency is again looking for a new executive, you'll find professionals eager to work in such a friendly agency and friendly community.

CHAPTER 14

So You Need Money

A primer for fund-raisers

THE FIRST TIME you're on a committee to organize a fund-raising drive, you'll face questions which never arise in private business.

How do you persuade people to give away money? How do you organize to solicit thousands of dollars? Are there proved methods? Can amateurs do it alone or should you hire professional money-raisers? If you hire professionals, how much should you pay?

You'll need solid answers to these questions, because the competition is stiff. In some cities the residents are exposed to six hundred national fund-raising campaigns and more than a thousand local drives per year—an average of four solicitations daily. All churches subsist on gifts. So do most hospitals, the youth movements, the privately supported colleges, all kinds of havens for handicapped, and scores of foundations for fighting disease. Philanthropy ranks as the fourth biggest United States industry in terms of assets; ahead of it come only manufacturing, farming and trade.

In terms of man-hours as well as money, begging is big business. Even a modest drive for church funds may take several hundred workers. Therefore the question of hiring a professional campaign organizer may arise.

Here is some advice on that question from David Church, executive director of the American Association of Fund-Raising Counsel:

> In a local campaign you don't need professional direction if you have a good volunteer leader. In fact, some volunteers have been through so many campaigns that they are almost as experienced as the professionals. But it will have to be somebody who can give himself to a project almost body and soul.
>
> When a professional is retained, it should be for a flat fee known to everybody in advance, and not for a percentage of the money to be raised. The fee is determined largely by the time required of the fund-raiser. In a fairly modest local campaign—say for a church or hospital—the professional's fee plus all general expenses should run between 5% and 7% of the goal to be reached. But in no case should his fee represent more than one-third to one-half of these total costs.

What will the professional do for his fee? He'll give you administrative help and technical advice. But he won't go out and ask people for alms, nor will he work at the multitudinous clerical chores which are a big part of the campaign. Anybody who dreams he can hire a professional and then sit back and watch the dollars cascade in is due for a shock.

Whether guided by a pro or by amateurs, here are the basic steps your fund-raising committee should take:

1. Line up a sponsoring committee of several dozen distinguished people whose names will add luster to your cause. The more civic, social and religious groups they represent, the better.

2. Set volunteers to work preparing cards with names of individuals and firms to be solicited. Each card should show address, phone number, and other pertinent data. Some organizations' card files are marvels of omniscience. They reveal not only how much the prospect donated to this or similar drives in the past, but how much "discretionary income" he probably has now; if he gets a

promotion during the year, the newspaper announcement of it is clipped and attached for evaluation to his card.

3. Organize the special gifts and the advance gifts committees. Use your wealthier people here, because these workers should tackle the big givers, and should be able to do so as personal friends. Impress on these committees that your goal probably won't be reached unless more than half of it comes from large gifts. Hat-passing and doorbell-ringing bring in only a dollar or two at a time.

4. Organize the corporate-giving committee, if there is to be one (and there should be, if this is a city-wide drive). It may have many subdivisions, depending on the number of industries, retail organizations, labor unions and other business groups on your prospect list. There may also be committees to approach the service clubs and churches and fraternal lodges.

5. Recruit the squads of workers who will make house-to-house calls, canvass by telephone, write letters, perhaps stand on street corners rattling a can. This is hard and discouraging work. Keeping this group gingered up is one of the keys to a successful campaign. Give it plenty of public praise, maintain constant touch with squad leaders, and use all your morale-building arts to see that they keep in touch with their squads.

6. Map the publicity push. You'll need a committee of publicity-wise people to write pamphlets and handbills, plant newspaper stories and pictures, wangle TV and radio time. Plentiful publicity—built around a striking slogan and perhaps a dramatic picture on a poster—can make an enormous difference.

7. Arm all your workers with facts. Prepare a campaigner's kit with answers to common questions and objections, reasons why the money is needed, specific ways it will be used. Personalize your facts. Stress what is done for John and Mary Doe through contributions, not how much or how many. Vivid details and dramatic stories are better campaign ammunition than

massive generalities, although you'll probably want to equip everyone with a few statistics.

8. Launch your drive with a loud bang. This might be a "kick-off meeting" at which workers get a fast, exciting sample of the kind of sales talk they should give to their prospects; it also is a good time to pass out kits, divide up the prospect cards, set quotas, bandy challenges back and forth.

9. Arrange for all your committees and squads to report at intervals of every few days. You might schedule "report luncheons" or the like. If well run, such report rallies can build a bandwagon spirit that keeps a campaign rolling and growing for a month or more. If poorly run, the meetings can deaden everyone's ardor. For detailed suggestions on planning and staging campaign gatherings, see Chapter 7.

Remember that the underlying secret of fund-raising is simply "getting enough people to see enough people." The person who is unwilling to give won't give, no matter what a solicitor says to him. And the person who is willing will give—if he is asked. Through sheer statistical probabilities, you'll always raise more money by asking more people.

The nine steps outlined here are means to get the asking done as widely as possible. Use imagination and horse-sense to fill in the broad outline with details to suit. And though the job may look tough, don't be afraid. Don't believe gloom-sayers who tell you, "People don't give the way they used to." The total of individual giving has multiplied tenfold in the last four decades.

Tools and tactics

Occasionally the authors of this book have worked as campaigners or consultants in a number of big and little fund-raising drives. From our personal experience, we'd like to pass along some suggestions which have worked well for us.

1. Set your goal cautiously.

It's a mistake to aim so high that your goal is unreachable. The prospect of failure will often discourage volunteer solicitors before they start. Most of the people in a campaign are already battle-scarred campaigners, knowledgeable about the size of the harvest they're likely to reap from ground they've been over before. Of course they probably err on the pessimistic side; many campaigns are poorly run, which means that many solicitors' past experience has not been rosy. A better-run campaign can surprise them with their own success. Nevertheless, if your goal is wildly unrealistic, or even seems so, your teams won't work as well as they would otherwise.

True, the size of your objective depends on how much is needed. But before you blueprint your needs, make a careful survey of the potential contributors, their past history of giving, and how much they can reasonably be expected to give this time. If your appraisal doesn't show a probability of getting at least 10 per cent more than you need, then you'd better lower your sights.

It's better to lower them before than after the campaign. A campaign which flops will mean a scarcity of volunteers next time. Therefore use ingenuity to find how you might get along with less than the amount originally set—at least for this year. Perhaps volunteer labor and/or donated material can reduce the size of the bank balance you need.

On the other hand, a sharp look around may show you untapped sources of contributions—whole groups you hadn't thought of soliciting. In any case, you must somehow crystallize your goal at an amount which will meet your needs yet also look attainable.

Having set your total goal, next break it down among the teams of campaigners. These team goals, too, must be carefully tailored to the prospects the team will solicit. A team must start with confidence in its own success.

The total of all team goals should be at least 10 per cent more than the campaign goal, so you can go over the top even if some teams fall short.

Team goals can be powerful tools in prodding your campaigners—especially if the teams are natural rivals. In a community-wide campaign, Kiwanis teams will battle mightily to outscore Lions or Rotarians. Bankers can be pitted against realtors or insurance men. If it is a church campaign, line up the Men's Club opposite the Young Married People and so on. For an in-plant campaign, the contest can be between departments.

In all such contests, scoring should be on the percentage of quota raised, not on the amount of money. The scores should be posted conspicuously—even ubiquitously; should be brought up to date every few hours if possible; and should be talked about and publicized with all the showmanship you can muster.

2. Go after pledges, not cash.

Americans prefer to pay in instalments. Not only do they buy homes and clothes that way, but they pay income taxes by monthly deductions from the pay check. Even on vacation they like "go now and pay later."

The churches learned generations ago to pass the plate every Sunday rather than ask for annual contributions. Now the Community Chest and other fund-raisers have demonstrated statistically that they can actually get a $24 pledge (to be paid $2 monthly) with greater ease than extracting $5 cash.

Sometimes you'll meet resistance when you first propose such a plan, but you can overcome it. We remember one plant personnel manager who told us, "You can't ask for pledges in this company unless you do the billing and collecting. No payroll deductions. We can't take on the extra bookkeeping."

We consented. So the personnel manager arranged a meeting at which we explained the pledge plan to employee team captains, in his presence. They agreed to a goal of one hour's pay per month per man. But when we described the mechanics of monthly collection, one man spoke up: "Why can't the pledges be deducted from our pay checks, instead of all this bother with monthly bills?"

The manager replied, "It's too expensive to set up deductions for little items like ten cents or twenty-five cents a month."

"How many men are you paying twenty-five cents an hour?" we asked him with a smile.

He smiled back. With no more ado, he agreed to payroll deductions of not less than $2 a month. The campaign in his plant showed a 300 per cent gain over the previous year.

In contrast, we went out to make a direct appeal to the employees of a garment factory, where about fifty women earn piecework rates and few are employed all year round. We again talked pledges. The boss evidently sensed some resistance among the women. He promptly told them the bookkeeper would be glad to deduct 25¢ a week for any who wanted to pledge. Again the campaign showed a gain.

A bus company refused to appoint a team or call a company rally, but did agree that the Chest solicitor could show up on pay day and talk to drivers individually as they came to the pay window. The stout-hearted solicitor stayed at the window tackling all comers for one long day. He got many refusals, and averaged only $3 apiece from those who did give. But a Chest leader persuaded him to try for pledges the next day. He immediately found himself signing up almost everyone, for $1 a month.

Of course monthly billing on pledges costs something—perhaps $1.20 if postage is paid both ways. And there is a shrinkage of about 2 per cent in the total of pledges fulfilled. But that still leaves around $22. As a rule of thumb, expect at least four times as big a haul—spread over a year, of course—if you campaign for pledges rather than cash. The difficulty is not so much in persuading people to pledge as in persuading your solicitors to ask for a pledge.

We recall one veteran campaigner who balked. But finally he gave in, after our indoctrination session, and did a fair job of presenting our sales pitch to his first prospect. At the climax he timorously asked the man whether he'd be willing to make a pledge. "Sure," the prospect said. "Put me down for a dollar a week."

"But that's fifty dollars a year," the amazed solicitor said.

"So what? They need it. I can spare it." From then on the solicitor lost his fears and turned in a tremendous total of pledges. Which points up our next piece of advice:

3. Train your solicitors.

Strangely, one of the hardest tasks in a fund drive is dragging the solicitors to a training session. It has been said that no one can be trained until he recognizes that he needs to be changed. Most people are loath to admit any such need.

That's why you'll hear such growls as "I'm willing to go out and raise the money for them. I've done it before. But I'm not going to waste time going to school like an ignorant kid." Yet the people who say this are the very ones who bring in a handful of small change instead of big pledges.

We helped organize a campaign in one city where many old-timers at first refused to attend training sessions, even though these were hopefully disguised as "sales meetings." The campaign chiefs agreed to make a stand on principle, and deny a campaign kit to anyone who wouldn't take training.

"In that case," barked one campaigner, "you'll have to get along without me."

"So be it," we said.

Fortunately he was the only hold-out. Another captain said his team couldn't come in for training, so could he take the kits to them? He compromised when we offered to go to their offices and give them orientation individually. Several others straggled in to the Chest headquarters at odd times and took the training singly. The rest of the four hundred solicitors showed up for group sessions, which lasted about an hour. Thus we convinced ourselves that solicitors will accept training if told they must, and given optional times to get it.

We've found that training is a must. Solicitors can't be counted on to explain the cause convincingly, and counter the various objections they'll run into, unless they are thoroughly primed. They also need schooling in the minutiae of filling in pledge forms and report envelopes and other paperwork. These should be simple, but you'd be amazed how much confusion the simplest forms can stir up if solicitors tackle them unrehearsed.

But the biggest value of training sessions is that they enable you to drill your solicitors in a tested step-by-step presentation to prospects. Get the best salesman or advertising executive in town to work up this presentation for you. Then put it into the form of a miniature flip chart which each solicitor can show to prospects.

Such a flip chart, familiar to admen and salesmen, enables your campaigners to say exactly what they should. They can refer to complete notes while seeming to talk naturally. One simple adaptation makes this possible: just put the notes on the backs of the cards—i.e., the side of the flip chart the prospect doesn't see.

These cards can be about eight by five inches, hinged at the top and bound with stiff cardboard covers, so they can be set up on a prospect's desk like a large letter A. The solicitor flips over the cards one by one, showing the prospect a series of cartoons or simple big-type statements. Meanwhile the solicitor sees his own notes on the other side of each card. These notes give him his complete patter—not word-by-word, which would sound stilted, but as an outline of key phrases. To help him sound expressive, you can even underline or capitalize the words he ought to emphasize.

Here is a sample. The first card shown to the prospect displays a red feather (the Community Chest emblem) and the simple legend: "1960 needs and the Fair Share solution." Simultaneously the solicitor's side gives him his own script:

Chest campaigning is not my REGULAR business, so

I'm going to use this FLIP CHART to be sure I keep on the track . . .

. . . save time for both of us.

The next card shows the prospect a cartoon of a harassed man beset by outstretched hands. It says, "There are too damn many campaigns in this town."

The solicitor's side says:

We DO have too many campaigns!

My firm [name it] thinks so . . . I'm sure you agree.

There are 33 agencies here . . .
(hand him "stamp" brochure)

We need them all . . .

We wouldn't live or do business in a city that didn't . . .

But we CAN'T have 33 campaigns . . .

My company believes they should be combined in one drive . . .

We are trying to get all businessmen to cooperate . . . to finance *all* agencies in one drive . . .

I'm here to ask you to help.

One campaign, to reach all your employees.

If you will come in with us . . . I'm here to help plan the campaign put on by your company.

How about it?

> STOP HERE. Don't flip to next
> card until he has agreed to a
> Company drive.

And so on through the whole routine, which takes a dozen cards. It's the most foolproof method we've seen.

4. Start soliciting at the top.

In most big drives, the bulk of the money is brought in by corporate campaigns. But there is a drastic difference in productivity, depending on whether or not the boss himself is interested.

If some lesser functionary takes total responsibility for organizing the solicitation in the plant, without being sure how the president feels, he and his team are bound to give it less push than if the president were strongly backing them. Sometimes they won't even open the door to the Chest unless the president tells them to.

The best way to line up the big boss is to persuade another big boss to talk with him. Equals listen to equals. Justin W. Dart, president of Rexall, is one of America's most effective volunteer money-getters because he personally goes out to other presidents' homes on Sundays to put the bite on them.

We recall one firm with three hundred employees which had never staged an in-plant campaign, and which refused even to give our solicitor an interview. When the solicitor reported his rebuffs, the local manager of Proctor & Gamble (a strong Chest supporter, by national company policy) said, "I'll talk to the head of that company. I know him." A few days later he spent two hours with the recalcitrant president—after which he told us to deliver the campaign kits to the president's secretary.

This didn't sound especially promising. If the president was still too busy to bother with us, how far could his secretary commit him? She took notes of the campaign procedure we recommended, and promised to call us when the president decided what should be done. We assumed we'd been brushed away again. But she did phone, weeks later. She asked us to stage our training session for the company's teams at a lunch meeting. There were about twenty employees at the lunch—which the company paid for—and their campaign brought in about $2,000. This from a company which had given nothing in past years!

One hotel, which we eyed hopefully as the scene of a proposed victory dinner climaxing the campaign, was reluctant to set a price which would make a large attendance possible. The secretary of the city's convention bureau called on the hotel manager.

"What we want," he told the hotel man boldly, "is a dinner for about two dollars a plate. I know you'll take a loss at that price, but—"

"I'm not interested," the other said. "We've given seven hundred dollars to your campaign, and another hundred toward subsidy for your report lunches."

"Let's think about it," said the convention man. "Suppose I talk to the men who furnish your meat and vegetables. If these are donated—and if you serve a chuckwagon type of dinner so you don't need a big crew of waiters—then maybe?"

He got the $2 dinner. Nobody but the manager himself would have dared make such a deal. Another restaurant also served a free steak dinner for a meeting of sixty oilmen to plan solicitation of their industry. This favor was asked by the chairman of the oil division in the campaign, who knew that many oilmen patronized the restaurant.

5. Open with a pilot campaign.

Before launching your big drive, you can crank up a lot of extra impetus by campaigning ahead of time in a few selected companies or organized groups. A squad of crack solicitors, fully alive to the importance of the cause, gives these prime prospects the works: an interview with the head of the organization to get him behind the drive, a tour by his teams of solicitors to see the welfare work in action, a rally or mass meeting of employees to hear a talk by the president, a push for pledges instead of cash, and a promise of a banner or plaque or other visible honor if the organization's quota is met.

The pilot campaign is being used by more and more Community Chests and United Funds, because results are spectacular. When publicized, it softens up other proprietors who have held out against permitting in-plant solicitation or payroll deductions. It also convinces solicitors that they ought to take training in the new solicitation methods.

Another surprising result of these demonstration drives is that many companies suddenly show eagerness to be "pilot" firms. Since only a few can be used as pilots each year, selection becomes a corporate status symbol.

6. Cash in on the urge to belong.

Psychologists say that the "feeling of belonging" gives a glow which almost everyone enjoys. The herd instinct is still strong. It can be used legitimately to keep a worth-while charity moving ahead. How? By forming "chapters" of the fund's campaigners wherever successful in-plant campaigns have been staged. Their team organization in a plant is thereby made permanent. Through the chapter, contributors are kept informed about what is being done with their contributions.

This means that when the time comes for next year's drive, last year's spadework need not be done again. Top management doesn't have to be resold; teams are already in being; last year's contributors don't need much resoliciting. Even enrolling new contributors is much easier.

The chapter plan also works well in professional groups. In Phoenix the Bar Association has signed 93 per cent of the city's lawyers to a pledge for $10 monthly contributions. Elsewhere barbers, dentists, doctors and beauty shop operators have organized charity chapters and stepped up their contributions. A few cities now use a plan whereby professional people sign an authorization permitting the Chest to draw a monthly check against their personal accounts for a stated amount.

Even amusement-park concessionaires, whom you might imagine to be too tough and worldly to take much interest in a Community Chest, can be moved to unbuckle their money belts. An amusement park usually has a business association of sorts. If the concession operators are herded into one room and shown the public relations advantages of pledging gifts as an association, they react as generously as anybody else. Their gift sometimes takes the form of an announced Community Chest Day, on which all concession profits for the day go to the Chest. Similarly, a pancake house in Long Beach, California, traditionally donates one days' proceeds to the Chest—about a thousand dollars.

7. Suggest an amount to give.

Motivation researchers have discovered that people feel secretly uneasy, when approached by a charity solicitor, because they don't know how much they ought to give. By an odd quirk of human nature, they don't want to look cheap—or foolishly overgenerous—in the eyes of even a strange solicitor. They would rather measure up to his expectation if they can. So if he shows them a table indicating how much is usually given by similar people (one day's pay, or a stated percentage of yearly income, or some other fair-share standard) they will probably give a bigger sum than they would otherwise.

Another point worth stressing by solicitors is: "For those in higher income-tax brackets, gifts cost less per dollar than for those in lower brackets."

8. Cultivate the elders.

Just because somebody is retired doesn't mean that he deserves no attention in planning a finance campaign. If you keep him on the mailing list, and keep in touch personally, he may surprise you.

One little lady, apparently about eighty-five, got off a bus in downtown Long Beach and plodded a block to the Community Chest office to hand a check over the counter. The clerk looked up the lady's card and found that she had given $20 the year before. On the point of expressing polite regret that this check was for only $5, the clerk looked again, and gulped. The amount was $500. The old lady remarked that she had just given an equal check to the Red Cross. "Now I can take a thousand-dollar deduction on my income tax," she said gleefully. Then she asked directions for taking a bus home.

Many a senior citizen, finding himself alone in life at the end of the road, has surprised some charity by bequeathing it his whole estate. Moreover, retired businessmen make valuable campaigners. Some astute fund-raisers form them into teams which seek big gifts between campaigns. These oldsters are good at it, because in many cases they ranked high in management and still have entree to mahogany row. They welcome an interesting, useful activity which renews their contacts.

9. Say thanks publicly.

Every donor, individual or corporate, likes to display some visible sign of beneficiaries' appreciation. Hence the paper poppies which war veterans' organizations place in your buttonhole; the "We Gave" stickers for windows; the engraved certificates and wall plaques and desk statuettes.

Beyond this, a donor enjoys seeing his name in print and his picture in the paper. Therefore the most successful community fund drives always arrange for local newspapers to print the names of people who give sizable amounts, and send a photographer to take pictures of big donors in the act of handing over a check.

Some organizations—notably churches and educational institutions—even publish booklets listing their supporters. The Century Club, an honorary organization of those who give $100 or more, is a feature of some campaigns.

A few people sniff scornfully at the "snob appeal" which they see in rewarding a donor by publishing his name. They feel that everyone ought to be content to do good in secret. It is true that most people will contribute, when asked, regardless of whether they get any thanks or recognition. Yet why shouldn't they be saluted for their gifts? We name parks and civic buildings after millionaire donors; can't we pay a fleeting tribute to smaller philanthropists? To be widely known as a benefactor is a form of "psychic income" which any generous contributor deserves to enjoy. Moreover, other potential contributors, seeing what he has given, may feel impelled to follow his example. Is this bad?

Corporations, too, cherish symbols of achievement. You may remember how many workers, from factory manager down to the assembly line, moved mountains in wartime for the right to flaunt the Navy's "E" banner on the factory flagpole. Today they will strive almost as hard for some bauble which betokens their civic-mindedness.

There was a striking demonstration of this in Long Beach. For years the Community Chest had awarded a bronze plaque (made of plastic) to firms which met a certain standard of fair-share giving for the corporate gift, the executives' personal contributions, and the employees' total donations. The standard was hard to meet, apparently. In fourteen years only fifteen plaques were earned. But in 1960 the solicitors talked it up when they approached business executives. What happened? Before the 1960 campaign was fully under way, thirty-six firms qualified for plaques.

One Long Beach furniture store sent in money and pledges which were only $12 short of the amount required for a plaque.

Through the

COMMUNITY CHEST

this Company supports these services for the use of its employees

Mr._____ of this Company will be glad to talk with you
if you or any of your family have problems in any of these fields:

FAMILY WELFARE

SALVATION ARMY

CATHOLIC WELFARE BUREAU

JEWISH FAMILY SERVICE

VOLUNTEERS OF AMERICA

FAMILY SERVICE

counseling on marriage problems,
parent-child relationships,
assistance in securing medical and legal aid;
health, old age and budgeting problems

HEALTH

VISITING NURSE SERVICE

Skilled nursing care in the home is available
on a part time basis to anyone, regardless of
economic status.

CHILDREN'S CLINIC

General out-patient medical care is offered
children from birth to 15 whose parents can
not afford private treatment by a physician.

PSYCHIATRIC CLINIC FOR CHILDREN

Diagnostic and treatment services are provided children 3 to 17 who present serious
emotional problems.

YOUTH SERVICES

for your sons and daughters

BOY SCOUTS • **GIRL SCOUTS**
BOYS CLUBS • **CAMP FIRE GIRLS**
CATHOLIC YOUTH ORGANIZATION
JEWISH COMMUNITY CENTER
YMCA • **YWCA** • **SALVATION ARMY**

Provides all age groups, all faiths, recreational physical, character building and citizenship training adapted to each age group.

ARMED SERVICES YMCA

USO

Provides service men a varied program of social, educational and religious activities. The program is provided near military units all over the USA and overseas.

TRAVELERS AID

Aid in formulating travel plans for inexperienced, handicapped or elderly persons entering or leaving the community.

CHILD CARE

DAY NURSERIES

Day care services are given children between the ages of 2-8 whose parent must work or where illness in the family prevents proper care of the child.

CHILDREN'S HOME SOCIETY

Places children of any age who are in need of adoption. Children are cared for in foster homes until placed. Counseling services are provided unwed mothers.

PACIFIC LODGE BOYS HOME

Provides care for boys, 10 through 18, who need special attention and treatment away from their homes.

A Chest official phoned the proprietor to thank him for his good showing and commiserate with him on missing the award so narrowly. The furniture man snapped, "I'm coming over."

Fifteen minutes later he burst into the Chest office with a $12 check—thereby winning a plaque which costs less than a dollar.

Another helpful way of saying thanks to a business firm is to send a poster listing the charitable works it is helping to support. When the Long Beach Community Welfare Council sent out such a poster, scores of firms phoned in for extra copies to tack on bulletin boards all over their premises. The poster is reproduced on pages 214 and 215.

In a covering letter, the chairman of the Welfare Council pointed out to employers:

> There undoubtedly are occasions when the work of one of your employees deteriorates because of personal problems outside. . . . I suggest that it would make for good employee relations if your employees realized that you are sympathetic to problems they face off the job. I suggest that you invite them to discuss such problems with your designated appointee. You can easily afford to do this because you have a staff of specialists as close as your telephone. You need only call the Chest office. They will give you the name of the proper agency to contact.

This served as a tactful reminder to all readers that they get a great bargain in the Community Chest: a city-wide network of welfare specialists and organizations, far superior to anything the biggest and most benign corporation could set up for employees if it had to pay the whole bill.

10. Consider affiliating with AID.

United Funds and Community Chests are organizations of agencies, holding combined drives to cut down campaign costs. The Associated In-plant Donors (AID) is an organization of givers, set up to cut down the number of plant solicitations—actually to eliminate all drives in their plants—and to give them the say as to where their contributions shall go.

AID contributions are handled entirely by payroll deduction. An employee is usually permitted to designate any charity anywhere in the country for his contribution. However, these specific designations are only a tiny fraction of the total contributed. The local AID board, acting for the employees, apportions the rest of the money between agencies as it thinks best. Usually a big share is assigned to the local Community Chest, with other large chunks going to national health agencies such as the Heart Fund, Cancer Society and the like.

Most Community Chests are enthusiastic about AID. This is only natural—because employees in AID contribute generously, the Chest gets a generous share, and there is no need to organize any solicitation of employees in AID plants.

In case of emergency

Suppose your fund drive starts with a mass meeting—in the middle of which, a rebel rises to protest that there should be no drive because the money isn't needed; because other causes need it more; these are troubled times and people can't spare the cash; the organization is poorly run and its funds are wastefully spent; and so on. It appears that he may stampede the meeting. What to do?

If you're presiding, give him a full and courteous hearing. Better to let him spout than to make a martyr of him by gaveling him down. When he finishes there'll probably be plenty of the faithful on their feet to answer him. If not, call on some well-informed and articulate old-timer by name, and ask him to comment. As a last resort, if you can't find anyone who makes a convincing reply, you'll have to undertake it yourself. Start with facts, then work into an emotional appeal on behalf of the people whom your organization serves. (Once your critic has had his say, don't let him heckle or rebut.) Then put the question: "Shall we go ahead with this campaign? Those in favor? Those opposed?"

It has happened—though not often—that a single loudmouth has virtually wrecked a fund drive at the opening meeting. This is more likely to happen if the cause is new, without much community backing yet. It can happen in an older organization when a few cranks or malcontents grab the floor and spread consternation among volunteers who were only half-sold in the first place. But it won't happen in your organization if you take a few advance precautions. (Remember, nine times in ten these precautions won't be needed; take a few soundings first to see whether they seem advisable.)

One precaution is to make sure that a convincing case can be made for your organization and its need of funds. Mentally put yourself through the worst grilling any enemy of the organization could give you; then plan how to answer him.

The next precaution should be to prepare a few shock troops to do this job of refutation, leaving you to preside impartially. You may even want to put them through a practice scrimmage of make-believe abuse.

Another precaution is to identify potential troublemakers and see that they're not invited to campaign meetings. Every movement has its flapjaws and foes of whatever costs money. Feel them out about the coming drive. Some may be for it, and will be tireless workers; such people often are. If they're against it, try to convert them. Then, if they remain rabidly opposed, you can explain that you're "sorry not to be able to count on them," so they won't feel affronted when they get no invitation.

If you're seriously alarmed about a big meeting, you can take a more drastic precaution: don't have a big meeting. Instead, just schedule a small separate briefing for each campaign team and committee. Give out kits and instructions in these private sessions, and make sure one of your storm troopers is there to give a rousing talk and counter any carping. Serve coffee and doughnuts. Some organizations prefer to start campaigns this way anyhow; it's more intimate and friendly.

What should you do if your fund drive gets off to a flying standstill, bringing in only a trickle of contributions the first week? Suppose your workers don't work? Suppose the drive nears the end and the goal isn't in reach?

Keep a few aces up your sleeve for such dark days. Perhaps you can get a big gift or two pledged in advance, but not announced, so you can give a dramatic lift to a sagging drive. Perhaps you can hold some crack organizers and solicitors in reserve, with the understanding they'll be thrown in as trouble-shooters.

If apathy is widespread, don't try to conceal the facts—but don't predict defeat, either. Instead try to create an atmosphere of crisis and determination, as Winston Churchill did in the worst days of the war with his "We shall never surrender" speeches.

As campaign chairman of the Los Angeles Community Chest drive in 1957, department store executive Walter W. Candy called newspaper reporters two weeks before the end of the drive to tell them that quotas weren't being met, and that he was calling an emergency meeting. "We can't wait until the last day," he said. "There's too much money still out. Each of the tens of thousands of volunteers working for this important cause must double his efforts." Then he announced plans for telephone round robins, reassignment of areas where leadership needed reinforcement, and deployment of special squads of fresh volunteers. The final fortnight of the campaign was a smash success.

If you're seeking ways to finance a community cause, remember that a massive sustained campaign isn't necessarily the only way. Particularly for smaller organizations, other techniques may be more productive. Let's consider some of them.

It pays to be different

A quiet, note-writing campaign can raise money. Get your members to send hand-written, personally addressed notes to everyone in sight. Here is one note which pulled well:

> Dear Mr. —————,
> The Family Service of Angelton is holding a membership drive and we are most hopeful that you will evidence your interest in the agency by becoming a member. Dues of $2 per year will aid in the Family Service program of an informed membership.
> I am enclosing an envelope and hope that you will honor us with your support and interest.
>
> > Sincerely,
> > *Mrs. William Fitz*
> > for Family Service

Instead of seeking money, an organization may do better to ask for donations of labor or materials. Many PTAs, YMCAs, Scout troops, service clubs and church groups finance themselves by rummage sales, paper drives, Christmas tree lots, cookie sales, pancake breakfasts and the like. We won't take space to detail their workings. You can easily find someone who has had experience with them. The key to their success lies in two facts: it's easier to get donations of material than of money, and it's easier to sell people something than to ask them for a cash handout.

On the other hand, collecting old newspapers or manning a Christmas tree lot or cooking pancakes for several hundred is heavy work. You need people ready to take off their coats and spend hours at physical labor.

Depending on your type of membership, you may find a better bet in a charity ball or a theater party or a benefit ball game. In big cities, an organization with socialite backing can make a quick killing with a charity ball. In one week in New York City, five parties in the grand ballrooms of expensive hotels netted $75,000.

These are spectacular affairs, requiring months of elaborate preparation by committees of society women (or sometimes by management of a big hotel). At San Francisco's Black and White Ball, shuttle buses carried three thousand guests between the ballrooms of four hotels, each decorated differently and providing different types of dance music. "Balls are fun, and the charities need the money," say the fashionable folk who attend.

Theater parties are spreading too. Actors dislike them because theater-party audiences talk more, cough more, and wander in and out incessantly. But producers and theater managers like them, since they sell big blocks of tickets. Many a charity likes them too, because its backers are more willing to buy tickets than to engage in other forms of fund-raising. The party is the thing, not the show. With tickets priced at $10 or more, thousands of dollars may be raised with very little work.

In Tucson, Arizona, a group of charity-minded sports enthusiasts extracts large sums from sports fans by staging benefit athletic contests. It got Tucson's four golf pros to put on an exhibition match; it persuaded the Cleveland Indians to play a charity game with the University of Arizona during spring training; all year round, it talks almost every amateur and professional star who comes near Tucson into joining one or another sports show.

A more unusual stratagem produced $3,200 for the First Methodist Church of El Monte, California. One Sunday the pastor told the parable of the talents, then handed out 185 bags containing money in the Biblical proportion of $1, $2 and $5. He asked his parishioners to use this money as they thought best, increasing it "according to your several abilities," and turn in the results six months later on Thanksgiving Sunday. One couple transformed a talent of $1 into $66 by baking and selling cookies; another raised $60 by making and hemming tea towels; another sold more than $75 in Christmas cards. One man painted a house with paint purchased in part with his talent. A dozen church members took empty bags and through self-denial and tithes built up their own talent. Everyone was willing to try, because the church committee had roused overwhelming enthusiasm for the plan to raise money for a new church sanctuary.

Here are a few more fine points which may be helpful:

Have your volunteer campaigners make their own contributions early, before the campaign starts. In that way they give you a sum which can be announced midway in the drive, if necessary, to push the total upward when it lags; they also set standards for giving, and are in a position to answer impressively when suspicious souls ask, "How much have you yourself donated?"

Send your campaigners out in pairs rather than alone. They give each other moral support, and make a stronger impression. Somehow two visitors seem far more important than a lone solicitor.

Finally, talk about the need, not the institution. Volunteers should ask support not for such-and-such a hospital, but for the health of the community; not for the Boy's Club, but for wholesome recreation for youth. This reminds contributors that their gifts will make things happen.

CHAPTER 15

The Root of All Evil

Ever think of embezzling?

IN ANY organization which handles money, people are sometimes tempted to tap the till. But most of the people serving charitable organizations are idealists and seldom think of these temptations. They're likely to let money lie unguarded. Therefore it behooves businessmen in the organization to make sure that proper business safeguards are installed.

One fund campaigner got an idea when a donor waved away a receipt because "my check is a receipt." This campaigner was taking in a lot of cash as well as checks. Of course he had to turn in duplicate receipts. But why make receipts for those who gave him checks? "Your check is a receipt," he told them. Thus he could turn in a handful of checks and a little cash, covering the total of his written receipts—meanwhile pocketing most of the currency. He got away with it for several campaigns before someone happened to notice how little currency he handed in.

Another fairly prominent businessman was soliciting large sums from wealthy people for a hospital. Because he was popular, careless donors wrote their checks to him personally. He couldn't resist the temptation. He began cashing a few checks and keeping the money. He wasn't detected until one big (and unreported) donor was reproached by a friend for "not contributing."

There have been cases of Scoutmasters and ministers leaving town with their organization's funds. Perhaps worse, honest men are sometimes under a cloud because the agency's accounting system leaves them open to suspicion, and some gossip starts a rumor that "Joe is making a good thing out of the organization."

Whether your group is large or small, its treasury—and its loose change en route to the treasury—should be carefully protected. All businessmen will agree that the following safeguards are a minimum:

1. Checks must always be made payable to the agency, not to any individual.

2. Solicitors in finance campaigns must always make out triplicate receipts (showing name as well as amount, and whether currency or check) and give one to the donor, another to the agency, keeping the third for their own records.

3. Payments from the organization must always be by check, not cash, and carry two signatures.

4. People handling considerable sums should always be bonded.

5. Agency accounts should always be audited, and the audit reviewed by a committee of capable people.

These are general rules of good business. The specific temptations arising from an organization's cash transactions and amateur accounting should be studied by experienced business managers, who will know how to install safeguards.

Strings attached

"Would you like some money for your foundation? Maybe there can be more later."

He groaned to himself, knowing what would follow if he accepted this obsessed offer. A first gift and then the next, then a place for Jim in the foundation, then why not on the board?

—*The Durable Fire*, by Howard Swiggett

Once in a great while, somebody who gives money to charity is concealing a selfish motive. A couple who send checks to an adoption agency may hope it will get them a baby. Contributors to a civic reform movement may be angling for gentle treatment by the reformers. A donor to a school may want to ease a dullard son past its portals.

Therefore it is well to glance at the teeth of a gift horse. If there are signs of more than benevolence, the net effect on the organization must be assessed. Maybe you can take the money anyway. Maybe you dare not.

The basic question to ask yourself is, Will the organization be compromised or committed to a harmful act? If a dairy wants to donate land for a camp, on the spoken or unspoken condition that the camp buy its milk from the dairy, there probably is no reason to refuse if the milk is good and fairly priced. But if the dairy owner expects to be elected president of the camp board, and could force his election once the camp is accepted, then you may be better off without the land.

Any civic organization errs greatly if it lets one person own it. Consider what happened to the Young Pirate organization in Bigburg. A retired merchant prince became president, underwrote a new headquarters building, and financed the whole professional staff. He moved his desk into headquarters and became the unsworn commander-in-chief. Until he died the Young Pirates never had community backing either in volunteers or donations.

While a large contributor seldom hopes for mercenary gain, he sometimes tends to become smotheringly possessive. More often, however, the domineering donor is someone whose drive has made him a force for good; his aggressiveness inside the agency may arise from his impatience with its weakness.

If your agency is smarting from the table-thumping of such a go-getter, perhaps you should ponder. Maybe your board would be wise to heed his grandiose-sounding advice. Big plans attract big backing.

The average heavy contributor, however, is likely to take a less prominent part in your movement than you would wish. Your problem is to persuade him to become more active, so he'll feel the loyalty that comes from being part of the inner guard. Even then he is likely to seek the background rather than the spotlight. "Don't name your camp after me," a business nabob told a charitable society recently. "If you do, people will think it's my private plaything. They won't be much interested in chipping in to develop it. Never tie up a whole project to one patron. Name one of the buildings after me if you like, then get others to finance your swimming pool and dining hall and so on."

Even small, unpublicized sums of money can get an agency into difficulty. For example, Family Service organizations in most cities have recently begun accepting fees of a few dollars from families in a position to pay for service they get. This policy looks logical, especially to business people who like to see social service become self-supporting when possible. But it raises new problems. A recent issue of *Highlights*, the national Family Service publication, reported as follows on a speech at its national meeting:

> Noting that budget committee members look with favor on an agency which meets a substantial percentage of its budget from charges to clients, Mrs. William Resnick decried the natural tendency to follow . . . with an insistent prodding of "why not more?" Becoming too fee-conscious may result in an agency's seeking, whether aware of it or not, clients who can pay—thus playing into the hands of those who criticize Family Service for not taking on multi-problem families . . . The dynamic agency's growth is unfairly restricted when fee income cannot be used to expand services but must be deducted from the budgets.

Trouble with the Community Chest?

The Community Chest was brought into being by volunteers, to meet a social need. Too many charities were competing for alms. By putting "all the begs in one askit," a community might raise more than if all agencies ran their own fund-raising drives. The giver would be solicited only once. The available volunteer force—which isn't limitless in most communities—wouldn't be spread too thin. Organizational know-how, and the economies of consolidation, should cut costs of campaigning.

For these reasons the Community Chest idea, which started in Cleveland in 1913, has spread all over the nation. Each local Chest is autonomous, and powerful. To qualify as a member of a Chest, a social agency must submit its budget to the local Community Welfare Council (an affiliate of the Chest), accept any revisions the Council recommends, and agree to conduct no separate campaign for operating funds. The Council appraises local needs and resources, straightens out overlapping of services, tries to spot and fill gaps in the charity picture.

Today only sixteen communities with population of 25,000 or more still spurn, the single, annual, collective type of appeal. But in recent years there have been rifts in the lute.

As one metropolitan Chest president points out, "The last twenty years have seen a race between explosive population growth, rising costs, and increasing Community Chest support. Our campaign here last year raised the largest amount ever, but still one million dollars short of minimum needs."

When there isn't enough money to go around, tempers get frayed. The Chest must decide where to pare agency budgets already cut in preliminary sessions. Thereupon the agency's supporters feel tempted to say, "Very well, we'll raise more money on the outside. If you don't like it, throw us out of the Chest. We may pull out anyway."

Personality conflicts often complicate the situation. A few professional Chest directors are nothing but ex-bookkeepers. Some long-established Chest boards and secretariats have grown a bit tyrannical. Likewise, some agency people throw their weight around to get a bigger slice of the Chest kitty.

A crippled child obviously has more appeal than an alcoholic; yet it may be as desirable to combat alcoholism as to support a children's hospital. Still, fund-bestowing and fund-dividing can be influenced by pressure groups.

Thus the budget committees of Community Chests and United Funds are nagged from all sides. "The gradual drift toward increased allocations to agencies with superior advertising power, high visibility and a more ready ability to go it alone, if necessary, is only partially due to lack of a carefully thought-out priority system," writes one agency president. "Social workers should provide agency board members with more facts and figures for use in budget committee presentations."

When there is antagonism between a Chest and one of its agencies, it is usually because one tries to coerce the other. If either the Chest or the agency commands, "You must, because we say so," then blood pressures rise. Everyone involved in such a test of strength—the Chest, the agency, and the community—is likely to get hurt.

The best way to avoid such bullying is to establish a framework in which the Chest and the agency must talk to each other as equals. If an agency is totally dependent on Chest financing, it is helpless. It will have to settle for whatever the Chest chooses to dole out—unless and until it builds up some outside income, and enough popularity to finance itself completely if necessary. Therefore an agency ought to do a continuous educational job, teaching the community about the services it renders, and cultivating its own private sources of fiscal strength.

Conversely, an agency may grow so popular that the Chest

drive would fail unless that agency were included. Or the agency's men on the Chest board may be so influential that the Chest would fail if they withdrew. Such an agency, by the mere threat of pulling out, can force the Chest to knuckle under to its demands.

Therefore a Chest should make sure its board is well balanced, with influential members representing all segments of the community, so they can keep the Chest going no matter who secedes. It must urge each participating agency to nourish community support of its own, so the loss of one strong agency wouldn't mean failure of the city-wide appeal.

To smooth over such squabbles after they arise is a far harder task. The principle is the same—to create an atmosphere of equality between groups which are unequal—but it takes broad vision. Somebody in the battle, perhaps everybody, will have to put the community first and the individual agency second. Somebody must persuade both sides to rethink their position, not from the standpoint of "who can lick whom," but "what is best for the community."

Another vexed question between agencies, or between the Chest and a member agency, is how much work the agency should put into the Chest campaign.

Some Chests expect that all the professionals and most of the volunteers in an agency will help solicit. This is a familiar chore for YMCA secretaries, health crusaders and other extroverted group workers—but how about the casework people, who deal only with unfortunates and hate to think of money?

The Child Welfare League of America says: "In the ordinary case, an executive charged with the operation of a social agency ought not to be expected to devote any great amount of time or energy to the financing of the agency." Many agencies would disagree. They might say that if an agency feels the Chest should do its money-raising, then the Chest is entitled to decide how much money it should have.

In almost every dispute between a federated fund and one of its members, there is much to be said for both sides. Beyond the advice already given, this volume would not presume to lay down rules for adjudicating or adjusting. Perhaps the best rule, here as elsewhere, is the Golden Rule.

Going it alone

Impressed with the spectacular success of the Community Chest in years past, many Americans now advocate another, greater structure: the United Fund. This would merge the Chest with all the national single-purpose charities in one immense fund-raising campaign for the city.

Some six hundred cities now run such united campaigns. But the big health crusades have resisted the idea fiercely, and the question of amalgamation has become a sort of philanthropic brawl. Several national organizations have coldly declined huge sums proffered to them as their share of the proceeds of a combined campaign. In at least one city, a United Fund got a court injunction to prevent an agency from conducting an independent drive for funds.

Sooner or later you may find yourself up against the problem of whether your organization should be inside or outside the Community Chest and/or the United Fund. Here is a brief summary of the major arguments on both sides:

The advantages of participation—

1. The agency isn't burdened with the complex task of organizing its own campaign. Its members will be expected to serve on speaking and soliciting teams, but this is nothing like the job of recruiting people and managing them.

2. A federated drive comes nearer to meeting its objective than would all the agencies on their own. In 1955 Pittsburgh had 129

organizations seeking funds in thirty-eight separate drives; only six raised the amount they needed. A year later a United Drive raised enough to fill the coffers of 102 organizations. "The little agencies meeting a quiet local need," said the chairman, "didn't get run over by the ones with the biggest bandwagon."

3. Campaign costs, in money and man-hours, are far lower in a federated drive. The Pittsburgh campaign cited above cost 4.1 per cent of the money collected—which was roughly half the aggregate cost of the multiple drives the year before.

4. There are unexpected dividends when business, labor and other community leaders get together for fund-raising. In Seattle the United Good Neighbor appeal led to successful campaigns for bond issues for a new civic center, a new public library, and school improvements. William M. Allen, president of Boeing Airplane Company and national chairman of the United Community Campaigns of America, commented: "Wherever a situation leads a community to focus on one objective and makes it work together, you score a gain in community spirit. If Seattle is now doing its job for libraries and civic centers and other aspects of a dynamic city, it's in a large measure because it has learned to do it for children's homes and family agencies and clinics."

The disadvantages of participation—

1. An agency getting all its support from a federated fund has no control of its budget. The budget committee of the Community Chest or United Fund must make arbitrary allocations of funds.

2. The agency loses its own financial friends. As President Eisenhower said, "True voluntary giving is based on the personal desire of an individual to make a private donation for a purpose with which he is familiar and which he wants to support." A donor to a vast general fund is giving to a much vaguer cause, and may therefore give less.

3. The agency loses most of its educational contact with the public. Without a campaign, it tends not to bother cultivating the public.

4. If and when a Chest or federation slumps, as its critics insist it will ultimately, participating agencies will be weak and almost friendless.

Regardless of the diplomacy usually exerted all around to avoid quarrels, the conflict of interest between a federation and the agencies is real and undying. There is a basic divergence in viewpoint and objectives.

The agency needs the active backing of people who know what it is doing. It cannot hold such support if it is financed by people who give to "welfare" rather than to its agency.

The Chest and the United Fund, contrariwise, need to protect the donors and campaigners from a multiplicity of demands. This can't be done if the agencies all run separate campaigns.

A man of good will, interested in helping his community, can only take one side or the other depending on his estimate of what is best for the purpose he has in mind. A line of reasoning valid in one community, or one agency, may be invalid in another.

Having chosen sides according to his lights, a man must then devote his best efforts to keeping peace in town, and minimizing the conflicts and handicaps inherent in either course.

CHAPTER 16

All Around the Town

Survey the scene

IN YOUR CIVIC CAREER you've probably already discovered that teamwork between organizations can produce miracles. An example picked at random is Mexico, Missouri, where a couple of businessmen pondered the sad fact that their town had no real facilities for recreation. They decided to do something about it. In the next twelve years the community built playgrounds, tennis courts, ball fields, a swimming pool, a golf course, an outdoor theater, and what one oldster described as "places where you can sit around talking to friends."

All this erupted because a few volunteers knew where to turn for help. Organizational resources are volcanic in every community if you know where to tap them. In the town of Mexico the original recreation-minded agitators got the Junior Chamber of Commerce to turn out with axes and shovels to clear ground for a multiple-sports area; the Kiwanis Club dammed a small stream to form a lake; Rotarians donated equipment for tennis, softball and basketball; women's clubs raised money for the amphitheater, PTAs for playground equipment; teen-agers converted an abandoned chicken hatchery into a youth center with furnishings provided by church groups. The local newspaper kept drumming up interest.

Evidently it pays to know your way around when seeking help for a community project. The better you understand the myriad movements and institutions in your city, and the warmer rapport you have, the more wonders you can work.

But to win their cooperation you should know their aims and methods and power hook-up. Therefore this chapter will give you a quick glance inside most of the major types of volunteer group. (Perhaps this chapter may help you not only in working with them but in deciding whether you might like to join them yourself.) The type of volunteer group least understood by outsiders is probably the fraternal lodge. Let's consider it first.

The mysterious lodges

Nearly all 248 major fraternal orders in the United States are secret societies, with rituals and passwords and handclasps. (The leading exception is B'nai B'rith, the largest Jewish lodge, which has no secret rites.)

All lodges' meetings, held at night in their own buildings or halls, are closed to nonmembers. Nobody can join spontaneously; he must be invited and voted on, and can be anonymously black-balled.

These mystic, benevolent orders are prosperous and populous. Estimates of their total membership range from twelve million to twenty million, with a good deal of overlapping. Yet fewer than 15 per cent of the dues-paying brethren show up at lodge meetings except on rare special occasions such as a New Year's Eve party.

Obviously the rank and file can never be mobilized in a community campaign such as a United Fund drive. On the other hand, a lodge often donates heavily to organized charities. Largesse in the name of the lodge, and from its treasury, goes to many varieties of patriotic, educational and recreational enterprises. So if you're raising funds, you may want to offer the brotherhoods a chance to chip in.

A lodge can sometimes muster a lot of manpower for a quick in-and-out operation such as a blood donor drive. It is often glad to arrange a Christmas party or Easter egg hunt for less-chance children. Its band and uniformed marchers appear at many public doings.

While the keynote of a fraternal order is good fellowship, its membership does include scores of two-fisted workers. Frequently a "task force" will help with canvassing in a community fund drive. The best way to arrange this, as suggested in Chapter 3, is to recruit a team captain who is a lodge member, and persuade him to recruit his team from his lodge brothers.

Lodges are keen on "taking care of their own." Welfare agencies sometimes don't realize they can get help for a needy person if there is a lodge affiliation in the family.

Every order has one or more pet uplift projects which it pushes. A survey of lodges in your community, to learn what their specific current strivings are, might be a fine contribution to your local inventory of resources.

When you set out to enlist a lodge's help, your first step must be to line up one or more members of the lodge. As closed fraternities, lodges seldom let in an outside speaker to advocate a project. But if an influential brother catches fire he can plead your case with key members, put it before the governing board, and finally urge it upon the assembled membership.

Service clubs: lunch with a punch

In any American community of twenty-five thousand or smaller, you'll meet a cross-section of its most consequential men at the weekly lunch meeting of any service club. There will be such men as the police chief, the president of the Chamber of

Commerce, a leading doctor or lawyer, a man who "owns half the town," the president of the ministerial association, the school superintendent, the commander of a veterans' organization, and so on. When they sit down together, things get done for the town.

Once a man becomes a lodge brother he is in good standing as long as he pays dues. But when he joins a service club he finds himself hooked for committee work, community boosting, and a regular weekly lunch. He must attend 60 per cent of the meetings or lose his membership. He must pitch in on projects or pay fines.

Service clubs may tackle almost anything: painting the women's club, promoting a new playground, a campaign for better library service, or a bus for the school basketball team.

They turn down ten appeals for every one they accept. As hardened businessmen, they know a poorly planned project when they see one. They also know, perhaps better than other groups, whether a proposal meets a real need in town.

The club treasury is seldom large, and is carefully budgeted at the beginning of each year. Appeals for donations seldom get far, therefore.

Manpower, not money, is the club's great resource. The keys to this steam boiler are (1) knowledge of a club's specialties and (2) regard for a club's wish to shine brightly and alone.

As service clubs grew in numbers they found themselves butting heads as workers for the same civic causes. This was painful and wasteful. Today there is reluctance to touch any project in a field staked out by another service club. But if you circulate with ears open, you'll know which club is most likely to get behind your project. You can usually enlist some club if you approach one which majors in that field, and approach it early enough to get included in the annual budget—and if you cater to its natural desire to be well known.

A cynic might assume that a club is chiefly interested in glory. He would be wrong. Clubs render most of their service almost secretly. Still it is true that club stalwarts, being human, get more excited about an idea which is distinctively theirs.

Nevertheless, service clubs can be induced to pull together if the work is so divided that each can play a unique role. For example, a Salvation Army summer camp got a club which was interested in child health to put up the camp hospital; another, which was sports-minded, to install a swimming pool and pay the pool staff; asking a third, which concentrated on slum kids, to provide camperships to send slum boys to the camp.

In angling for service club support, approach it quite differently than you would a fraternal order. Your appeal should be made by a speaker from your own organization, not a member of the club. They welcome an outsider with a new voice and a new story. To get him a preliminary hearing before the club's board of directors, a simple phone call to any prominent member may suffice.

Your speaker should be both persuasive and well armed with facts. He won't get a quick endorsement, because the board is importuned by so many. However, any truly useful project in the club's own field has a good chance of ultimate approval.

That approval must come from the assembled club itself, rather than the board. So if the board gives the green light, it will expect you to send a speaker to the weekly lunch meeting. He should be stirring, logical, and preferably a bit amusing withal. Fulfill these expectations, and you'll see the massed and disciplined power of a service club move mountains in your behalf.

The veterans seldom change

The American Legion, Veterans of Foreign Wars, and other ex-soldier groups are aging, dwindling, and perhaps mellowing—but they still are potent in community life.

They stress activities to solidify their feeling of a common heritage and brotherhood. Unless a community project has a shining patriotic aspect, a post is unlikely to get fired up about it.

Their membership is drawn from all income levels, rather than from management echelons as in the service clubs. They're not in touch with the needs of the city as a whole. But they are keenly aware of family needs. They are strong family men for the most part, and warmly sentimental about the woes of a family. They are also boyish and sports-loving, so their civic interests often center around juvenile ball teams, programs for handicapped children, and recreation for soldiers and sailors on leave. One-shot welfare operations—baskets of food at Christmas, for example—may get a strong helping hand from the veterans.

The strength or weakness of a veterans' post equates closely with the caliber of whoever happens to be commander that year. A strong commander can rally many men to the support of a cause. A weak one seems to anesthetize those under him.

Therefore you'll be wise to put your proposition to the commander himself. If he likes it, he may ask you to explain details to his board or to the membership—but he's the only one who can do the real selling.

What was said about highlighting a service club's identity applies also to a veterans' post. Nationally there is hot rivalry between posts, so a post likes a project which makes it better known and loved, and can be reported impressively.

Womanpower and youthpower

"Never underestimate the power of a woman," a national magazine has been telling advertisers for years. And never overlook the potential of women's organizations when you're seeking support for a worthy cause.

A little-known organization, the Needlework Guild of America, "the charity that helps other charities," gives 1,100,000 articles of new clothing and linen to the needy every year. They never see, or even choose, the beneficiaries. They give the goods to local agencies and institutions, relying on them to distribute the gifts.

The multitudinous good works of the Junior League, the women's club, the women's auxiliaries of medical societies and veterans' posts and churches—all these are known to people familiar with grass-roots community work.

Less well known are the quiet enterprises of 1,200 local groups of the League of Women Voters. They are the only nonpartisan national movement which specializes in trying to make local governments run better. Don't forget the League if there's a clean-government fight to be won at city hall or the state capital.

Youth organizations, too, can be powerful allies. They have supplied attendants for public museums; done chores in hospitals; procured, painted and donated public trash baskets; drawn up and enforced safe-driving codes; helped plan and build recreation centers; fought racial and religious discrimination.

The trick of getting adolescent participation is to work with them, not for them. Bring them problems rather than solutions. You may offer suggestions, but let them figure out their plans themselves. They may surprise you most pleasantly.

Nothing but culture

There are many nonprofessional theater groups in the United States, and their number is growing at an astounding rate. In 1956 two thousand cities and villages had community theaters. In 1960 there were thirteen thousand.

Even though your own interests may be far removed from theatricals, you may find that your town's theater group can help with other civic enterprises. When the church in Hyde Park, Vermont, (population 1,291), needed a new furnace, the Lamoille County Players put on a charity operetta. The proceeds paid for the furnace. Many a Little Theater sends touring groups to give free performances at hospitals, orphanages and Army camps.

The neediest cultural enterprise in town is usually the public library. On the average, it struggles along with one-third the funds needed for minimum standards of community service. But if you're eager to improve the library in your community, you can turn to the Junior Chamber of Commerce for help. It's eager to. Its world conference in Tokyo adopted Operation Library as one of the organization's major projects.

It is surprising what gifts are forthcoming when business, labor, and the wealthy get interested in improving the cultural tone of their community. A bright example of this is Flint, Michigan.

Some years ago Flint was a grimy factory town where thousands of unskilled workers lived in shabby shacks that nearby communities called Shantytown.

Today the slums have given way to parks and playgrounds. The city has a symphony orchestra. There is a magnificent art gallery, a civic theater, even a planetarium. Soon there will be scientific and historical museums, a swimming pool and a music center.

It all started when a retired industrialist, Charles S. Mott, became interested in opening the schools as recreational centers in the evenings. With that started, he grew more fervent and helped organize a committee of two hundred which met weekly to plan for the march of culture in Flint. In the last two decades the committee has raised nearly nineteen million dollars from local factories, families, unions and clubs.

This is what volunteer teamwork can do for a city. If it can happen in such a dreary, dispirited place as Flint once was, it can happen anywhere.

The people's choice

Citizens elected to part-time, virtually unpaid public office in such bodies as the board of education or the city council are in for a rough ride—because they spend taxpayers' money. And yet costly civic improvements can be made if the planners know how to round up community support. The key is simple:

Work *with* people, rather than *for* them.

In Setauket, Long Island, school bonds were rejected three times. Then a couple of members of the local civic association began quietly asking people, "What do you think we can do about a better school? What sort of improvements should it have? How big? What would you be willing to pay?"

After weeks of such groundwork, the civic association called a public meeting to which it invited representatives of thirty business, church, and social organizations. There committees were set up to study every aspect of the hypothetical new school—how it should be designed, what materials should be used, and so on. After six months of study, a $634,000 school bond carried by an easy majority.

Princeton University's bureau of urban research says, "One recurring motif is that city planning requires increased public participation if it is to be most effective."

That thought might be the theme of this whole book. Democratize! Get more and more people interested and involved. Link up with as many organizations as possible. Ask individuals for their opinions, then for their help. They're eager to give it, but they're all too seldom asked. As Dr. Woolf of Columbia University says, "There is an unbelievable amount of good will available."

Casework: to be continued

Someone once asked a bishop, "Do you like the Salvation

Army?" He replied, "I cannot say that I do—but to be honest I must confess I believe God does."

The Salvation Army, like many other religious and secular casework agencies, is doing God's work in the service of the poor, the unloved, even the unlovable outcasts. Casework is an especially foggy frontier of community betterment. You may want to be at least sketchily informed about it.

Any agency formed to help individuals rather than groups is seldom making visible progress toward a visible goal. It has no particular quotas; no plans for altering the civic scene; no big projects which can start with a fanfare and finish with a flourish. Therefore their board members and committee people often feel superfluous—and their treasuries are chronically emaciated, because a casework agency can't dramatize itself as well as other types of organization can.

Nevertheless, if you know a family, an individual, or a category of people who need help in a hurry, a phone call to the right casework office may start things happening in their behalf. Moreover, if you ever work in a community fund-raising drive, you'll do a more persuasive job if you know something about the impressive services rendered so quietly by the caseworkers who depend on you for funds. So here is a quick look at some common kinds of case work.

A Catholic, Jew or Mormon can usually get counsel and succor from welfare organizations operated by his church. There is a Catholic Family Service and Jewish Family Service in nearly every sizable city. The Mormons—known more formally as Latter-day Saints—keep storehouses full of food and clothing; own and operate farms, canneries, mills, factories and salvage shops. They can offer a wide variety of jobs to unemployed church members.

The Quakers (officially the Friends) and some other Protestant sects do a great deal of welfare work among needy people, not necessarily of their own creed.

Such missionary societies as the Salvation Army, the Volunteers of America and other missions on skid row are interested in soul-saving, but they soft-pedal this while exerting themselves to help bums, ex-convicts, prostitutes and other unfortunates pick themselves off the pavement. They run maternity hospitals, place children in foster homes, provide low-cost residences for working girls in cities. They gather household discards and use them to provide self-supporting rehabilitation work. They train human derelicts and help them find jobs.

The busiest and farthest-flung instrument of privately financed mercy is, of course, the American Red Cross. Unlike most welfare agencies, it relies not so much on professional social workers as on trained volunteers.

Its blood banking, its aquatic training, first aid courses, home nursing, mother and baby care, gray ladies in hospitals and other programs keep enormous numbers of people working for free. Meanwhile these volunteers undergo training so that they can step in efficiently if disaster strikes.

Because of this unpaid help, the Red Cross holds operating costs to 13¢ for every dollar spent. Fund-raising costs consume only 4 per cent of the millions disbursed yearly by the national headquarters and the 3,700 local chapters. This is remarkably low, in comparison with costs reported by most other voluntary charities.

CHAPTER 17

The Convention: Underside View

Before you start

SUPPOSE that you are to be in the Midwest on a business trip next month; that the annual meeting of the Pro Bono Publico Association of America is scheduled for Chicago at the same time; that you are a member of your home city's Pro Bono board; and that you are asked to be a delegate to the national meeting. Should you say yes?

A decade ago, most men would have agreed offhand. They would have assumed (almost always correctly) that acceptance wouldn't entail work. But today, if they're smart, they don't accept unless they're ready for some hard labor.

The old-time convention with many orators, meaningless committee reports, and inert audiences is disappearing. From the American Legion all the way around the spectrum to the Audubon Society, nonworking delegates are becoming *personae non gratae.*

As a delegate to our imaginary Pro Bono Publico convention, or almost any other, you assume a burden. You will be expected to say something intelligent during floor and committee discussions, and carry back valuable information to your home constituency.

To accomplish these missions, forearm yourself. You must find answers to this twofold question:

"What will my presence at the convention accomplish (a) for the national movement? (b) for our local branch?"

You may be helpless to make the tiniest dent on the national movement if its officialdom is entrenched and contented. This is worth investigating before you decide whether to attend.

However, assuming that the Pro Bono convention will be receptive to new ideas, your problem is to gather up whatever fresh facts and ideas can be found in your local organization, and present them forcefully to the national meeting. Has your chapter a reform to propose, or a demand to push? Has it a new technique or insight which other chapters need? If so, inform yourself fully.

What you bring back to the local branch will depend upon what it needs. Perhaps it needs specific information, or solutions to a problem. Or perhaps it needs a new professional; the best in the movement will be at the convention, and some of them will be alert for feelers.

Perhaps your group wishes to form certain alliances. Perhaps it merely wants to avoid the ill-will to which absentee groups are liable. Perhaps it seeks good speakers for its own meetings, or for regional gatherings. Perhaps its only desire, in urging you to attend the convention, is that you will be infused with more pride in good Pro Bono Publico.

Whatever its needs and desires, fix them in mind before you accept the invitation. *Write yourself a memo defining your goals.*

Your next step will presumably be to get hold of the agenda, and a list of speakers and committee chairmen. People who can help you may be on the list. By writing ahead and explaining your problem, you may arrange to talk with them privately.

Perhaps plans for the program are still fluid enough so that you can write to the planners with a proposal for a speaker, topic, or type of program you think should be included. If the agenda is already set, it can guide you in shaping questions and comments you should have at the tip of your tongue.

Your preparation, if you are in earnest, may also include reading up on previous conventions. You can profit by going over their programs with men who attended. At the least you will get tips about certain people to look for, or to avoid. Reports from last year's delegates may suggest further questions. What was done as a result of last year's convention? What should have been done but was not? Has anything been written subsequently on the convention topics of interest to you?

You may wish to review the Pro Bono constitution. Knowledge of it is a handy weapon in convention skirmishes. The compleat delegate carries copies of the constitution into all sessions.

If you are one of several delegates from the local group, your preparations will include a preliminary meeting with them. The delegation obviously should work as a team. Information to be gleaned, people to be met, meetings to be attended and reported on: all these can be parceled out in advance.

Your briefing should include information about the kind of people you will encounter at the convention. Our fictitious Pro Bono Publico Association may be a monolith of near-identical clubs or chapters, such as Rotary or Red Cross. On the other hand it may be a conglomerate such as the American Association for the United Nations, or the White House Conference on Education. If so you will find yourself among a miscellany of church groups, diplomats, business associations, lawyers' committees, international labor organizations, group work and casework agencies and umpteen others.

Send in your registration as soon as you agree to attend the convention. There are many convention situations in which the early bird gets his proverbial reward. If you are asked to order tickets, sign up for special events, or indicate any choices, do so as early as you can.

It is likewise prudent to make hotel reservations far in advance, if convention authorities are not assigning rooms. For a big convention, a year ahead is not too soon.

If your family is to go with you, this calls for further planning. Are convention authorities arranging to keep families amused while fathers are in meetings? How will the family spend the evenings?

Months before a big convention, train and plane reservations are sold out around the convention dates. Your long-range plans should include buying round-trip reservations at the same time you book hotel rooms.

One more step should complete the preliminaries: Make sure your local group knows how to reach you at the convention, in case something important arises after your departure. And take along the local phone numbers, in case you want to call back for consultation.

The delegate's first hours

Civic-betterment conventions are seldom as smoothly run as business conventions. Therefore the forehanded delegate will busy himself, between the time he arrives and the first gavel falls, with such moves as these:

1. As soon as he receives his room key he hastens to the room and establishes tenancy. Probably he unpacks completely. He phones the barbershop for an appointment if he hopes to get a haircut at any time during the convention. He sends clothes out for pressing if they need it, but holds enough clothes to get him through thirty-six hours. Valet service at these conventions is unpredictable.

2. He ferrets out room numbers of everyone he intends to interview. This is a good time to phone them and clinch a few appointments for the off-hours.

3. He registers with convention authorities, checks his voting eligibility, and makes sure he gets identifying badges. Otherwise he might be delayed or blocked altogether in trying to enter a meeting.

4. He signs up for whatever dinners and other special gatherings require advance reservations. This sometimes is the only way to make sure he will get in.

5. If possible he gets a copy or two of the convention program. Sometimes only a few extra copies are printed, and a delegate who loses one cannot get another. Therefore a provident conventioneer writes his name and room number on his program, marking it *Please return*.

6. To save useless note-taking, he asks if there is a handy press room where he can get mimeographed copies of convention talks. He also inquires whether any local newspaper offers a service which will mail home its entire coverage of the convention.

7. If there is a list of delegates and guests, he looks at it. He may see familiar names he did not expect.

8. He makes advance plans to avoid being ill-fed. This may involve arranging for room service, or reconnoitering for good restaurants he can reach quickly by taxi. He knows that every nearby eating place will be jammed.

9. He arranges his post-convention getaway to avoid entrapment. The grapple for porters, bellboys, cashiers and taxis sometimes lasts for hours after adjournment. Perhaps he plans to stay over until the next morning. Or perhaps he arranges to pay his bill in advance and get his bags down while the final session is still going on.

Delegate in action

With the convention at full blast, an active delegate may feel like a cork in a washing machine. He'll be tempted to let himself bounce around, doing whatever comes naturally.

But this isn't the way to be an effective delegate. He must try to do several things which may not come naturally.

Separate from your home-town friends. A delegation which moves en bloc misses a lot. Each of your delegation should eat with different groups at every meal, scrape acquaintances, roam the corridors and lobbies instead of lounging with the home crowd.

Keep a list of new acquaintances, their home addresses, their room numbers at the convention. Far-flung contacts within a national organization can pay off in unexpected ways.

Cast a sharp eye on agency professionals—just in case. Your local agency may be perfectly staffed today yet have a vacancy tomorrow. Keep a list of the bright pros who might fit into your organization some day. And make friends with them now. Years later, one of them may remember your friendliness to him at a convention.

Calculated gregariousness and inquisitiveness are always in order at a convention. Talk shop in the corridors, on sightseeing tours, on the golf course, at parties. These are chances to pick up gossip which never gets into the transcript yet may be important for its sidelights on the whole movement.

Since one learns more by listening than by talking, the best conversational gambit is to ask a question. You may justifiably feel that your local organization is doing the best—or worst—job in the country, but suppress the urge to tell all about it at the convention.

Convention speeches are often meaty though dull. The dullness arises from monotonous delivery, rambling organization, or technical jargon. Still the meat can be readily extracted if you take some trouble. For example:

1. Make inquiries about a speech beforehand. Advance copies, or at least summaries, are often available.

2. Make inquiries about the speaker. If he is said to be lively,

you may want to attend even if his subject does not interest you. One of your roles is talent scout for good speakers for your local meetings.

3. If you know that a speaker will discuss a subject important to you, try to take along an advance copy of his speech and read it as he talks. You can underline key points which might be missed in listening alone. His voice and gestures may clarify an opaque paragraph. You can also jot questions in the margin.

4. With or without manuscript, try to accompany the speaker in thought. Keep asking silent questions. What is he likely to say next? Where is his train of thought headed? Are there flaws in it?

5. As he talks, keep your local problems in mind. What he says may give clues to a solution.

6. Note-taking is essential if you haven't a transcript and want to get anything out of the speech. Vivid as it seems now, you won't remember next year.

Where should you sit at a convention session? If you may want to leave before adjournment, sit near an exit. If you hope to speak, sit near a microphone. If you arrive late, have pity for those coming still later; don't block them by standing in a doorway or aisle.

Will you speak from the floor? If there are no microphones, talk in a dignified bellow. And instead of facing the chairman, turn toward the bulk of the audience, so as many as possible can hear. Remember, too, that you'll be tempted to talk at length. Don't! Be brief.

Volunteer for committee assignments and other extra work at the convention. The volunteers are the ones who become insiders.

Don't try to get much sleep at the convention. You can catch up later. For now, resolve to burn the candle at both ends. Late-night bull sessions are vital and should not be neglected. Early rising is also important, to be sure of getting a good breakfast before the mob surges in.

It is good protocol to mention your name and your city in greeting conventioneers you have met before. It not only spares them possible embarrassment but leads them to reciprocate.

Adolescents have conventions too, and some adults must attend to ride herd. Anyone doing so may be interested in the words of a young man who turned permanently hostile to a certain youth movement because of an experience with its adults. "I have no use for the men in that organization. When I was a teen-ager two of them took a crowd of us to the convention. As soon as we went to bed at night they'd go out on the town. Then in the morning we couldn't get them up, and we didn't know what we were supposed to be doing. Their movement is no good."

Kingmakers, steamrollers, and minority rule

There are tactics through which a small determined clique sometimes tries to rig or undermine a convention. For example:

The Stall: The chairman starts a meeting late. Speakers use more than allotted time. A few delegates hold the floor, wrangling over trivia until others walk out in boredom. Then the late-staying insiders whisk their plan through.

To counter the Stall, fight for a limit on debate. Or demand that the vote be postponed until another meeting. If balked, try to persuade your adherents to stay to the bitter end. If balked again, raise a point of order regarding lack of a quorum; minority actions may be invalid under the organization's constitution.

The Steamroller: The chairman ignores delegates who want to talk on one side of the question. Or he cripples them with a time limit—one minute per speech, perhaps. In preparation for this latter maneuver, the forehanded minority has broken down its argument into a series of hard-hitting one-minute blasts, arranged in logical order.

To block the Steamroller, oppose any unfair time limit on speakers. Point out the vast advantage to a bloc which is well prepared. Fight for longer talks, even if there must be fewer; you can argue that this consumes no more total time. Then demand a recess to give your people a chance to prepare their speakers—which the other side has doubtless already done, as you can remark.

If a chairman recognizes only speakers from his own side, become a polite nuisance. Demand recognition in louder and louder tones. Draw the meeting's attention to the fact that it is being steamrollered. In a big convention this may mean forcing your way to the rostrum. While doing so you can conceivably become disheveled or worse. Whether you risk it depends on the importance to you of the question at issue.

A last-ditch counter available to a large group is to walk out en masse and appeal to stronger authorities. Pass a petition among the delegates, circularize the national membership, appeal to the newspapers or the courts.

The Filibuster: Used when a chairman is not part of the plot but is irresolute or handcuffed by rules. A minority paralyzes a meeting and prevents action by holding the floor.

To break this up, send a note to the chairman pointing out what is happening, and suggesting he cut off the speaker. Offer to stand up so he can call on you. When you get the floor, demand an immediate vote or at least a limit on debate. If no motion is pending, make one.

Sometimes a chairman is too timid to interrupt a filibuster. Your recourse is to make the interruption yourself without waiting for recognition. If the chairman rules that the speaker can hold the floor indefinitely, then you have lost unless by heckling or by circulating notes you can induce the majority to walk out and hold a rump session.

The Quick Opener: A petition is unexpectedly produced and rapidly circulated. Or postcards appear on every chair, needing only signatures for mailing. Or somebody offers a harmless-sounding proposal that wasn't on the agenda. "This isn't very important," he says, "but it needs immediate action."

To counter this, ask "Why isn't this on the agenda? Why must we act immediately? Can't we think it over a little?" Rapid deployment is the best defense against devices for massing signatures behind a minority scheme. Get your people out to spread warnings wherever the petitions are. Send a "truth squad" to accompany and refute them. Or move around with counter-petitions.

The Blitz: A quick passing of the hat is its common form. A speaker makes an electrifying appeal, collection plates swiftly appear on the aisles, and shills pull out their wallets to start the money flowing. Other manisfestations are the ostensibly spur-of-the-moment parade, strike, or demonstration. Nine times in ten, any sudden emotional action by a big meeting is contrived in advance.

To counter it, ask loud blunt questions. "How will this money be spent? How do we know this is on the level? Why are you trying to rush us? What are the facts?"

If the chairman won't recognize you, or you can't make yourself heard, move through the group and buttonhole as many people as you can. Talk loudly enough so that everyone near can hear. The way to break down mob psychology is to challenge individuals.

The Misleading Summary: To close a discussion, the chair or someone else summarizes it rather differently from the sense of the meeting. There are cheers and handclapping.

This trick is often worked at the end of a dull meeting. Somebody offers a resolution or calls for action which overrides majority sentiment. The well-distributed minority makes the room shake with applause, and the motion is whopped through, After a quick adjournment the dazed majority drifts away, each man thinking to himself that he must be out of step with everyone else; the meeting didn't go the way he thought it had, because the last speaker evidently voiced majority feeling. This illusion can do a lot of damage if it gets into the record, or filters out to other parts of the convention.

Your riposte is to prevent adjournment. Challenge the summary. Wake up the majority and prolong the debate. Demand a vote by secret ballot if the situation demands it.

Closely allied to this is the *Phony Ovation* for a candidate. Kingmakers at a convention try it often. Their claque makes maximum possible noise on behalf of their candidate, hoping to convince everyone that he's overwhelmingly popular. You can't do much about this, except call attention to it in public statements soon afterward so that everyone realizes what was really happening.

Two obvious and time-worn tools of dirty politics are the *Smear* and the *Straw Man*. Somebody spreads a bad rumor about a rival. Or somebody props up a bogey man—Communism or the Ku Klux Klan, perhaps—and attacks it fiercely, implying that his rivals are secretly behind it. Answer such slurs as fast as possible, before they spread any farther than you can help. Rush your truth squads around wherever they're needed. But don't get too excited, or seem too alarmed. It's better to appear contemptuous and half-amused when somebody slings mud at you. Many times you can afford to ignore it entirely.

An equally old but dangerous trick is the *Snap Vote*. Sometimes a chairman in cahoots with a minority finds that his group has a temporary majority, because some of the other side are absent. He calls for an immediate vote on a crucial matter. Here's where your knowledge of the organization's rules may help. If there isn't a quorum present, you can block a vote by calling attention to this. If there is a quorum, or the by-laws don't specify what constitutes a quorum, then you'll need other parliamentary tactics to delay the vote: offering a series of amendments to the motion, prolonging debate as long as possible, calling everyone's attention to the absence of your cohorts. Should these tactics fail, and you see your opponents will carry their motion in spite of you, then vote for the motion yourself! Why? Because then you're legally entitled to move for reconsideration of the motion later, when your side regains the majority.

The Double Agent can throw any convention into confusion. For a vivid description of this ruse, see Eugene Burdick's novel *The Ninth Wave*, Chapter 24. Briefly, the idea is to ruin a candidate or cause by pretended support—support which is so rabid and obnoxious and unfair that it repels people. To counter this, you must disavow the support promptly. After repudiating such an "ally" you must work hard to neutralize his sabotage by sane and temperate talk, drawing the sting out of everything he said. It isn't easy. Think fast, and play for time, if you find opposition agents pretending to side with you. Don't let them stampede the crowd into a sudden decision.

CHAPTER 18

The Convention: Topside View

Conventions with a difference

LET'S SUPPOSE you've agreed to be chairman of the state or national convention of some far-flung organization, either the club type or agency type as defined in our opening pages.

Presumably you want to make your convention a bit different. You may have been to many which were stupefyingly alike. There was the opening session filled with oratory. Then there were committee reports to which nobody listened. Then there were long, long section meetings in stuffy rooms.

It used to be standard practice for convention speakers to read manuscripts in a drone, hardly ever sneaking a glance at their audience. Delegates sneaked away before each speech, or ambled out boldly in the middle of it.

Every committee was accustomed to deliberate amid clouds of tobacco smoke and squeaks of portly delegate bodies on small collapsible chairs. Delegates plodded into the same beflagged and beflowered banquet hall for the same final ordeal: to stare at an elongated speakers' table while dignitaries told their life stories.

Such a convention is an atavism now. Most civic groups have thrown out the old convention pattern of statistics, platitudes, honeyed welcomes and time-killing. Showmanship and pragmatism are in the ascendant. Even the ventilation and the chairs are better.

This year's conclave is expected to be new and bright and different from last year. So if you are a convention planner you presumably need a large number of novel ideas. The Friday session should be different from Thursday. Each hour should bring a change of pace.

Here are a few innovations which have proved successful:

The Speechless Convention. Instead of speeches it uses playlets, mock trials, quiz shows, make-believe press conferences.

The Mystery Voice. Someone with a quick wit but no venom is posted out of sight with a microphone, ready for friendly corrective heckling whenever the talk gets trite. His identity is a secret. He can needle prolix speakers into brevity and lucidity.

The Convention Handbook is a printed notebook, probably loose-leaf, with questions on one page and blanks on the facing page for a delegate to write his own answers. The questions are those which a speaker is expected to answer, and which panels and sections are expected to thrash out.

Closed-circuit Television costs about $1,500 per hour per city. Maybe you should consider it. Your members can thereby attend your convention without leaving home. Some organizations have tried this, and liked it. Listeners say they see and hear better, and feel much closer to the speakers. Of course there should be two-way hook-ups (voices only) for question-and-answer periods.

Small Discussion Groups. (Often called buzz groups in social work.) If your section meetings and committee meetings are likely to be unwieldy, with too many people trying to talk, you can split them into subgroups of six or eight members which report back when the main group reassembles. This is how the White House Conference on Education was handled a few years ago. Any public librarian can help you find detailed descriptions of its workings. It was divided into dozens of small panels, each considering the same question at the same time. Reports were bucked up to higher panels. Thus every delegate had ample chance to talk, and every worth-while idea could fight its way up the pyramid.

Theatrics. You can hire a professional group, or rehearse a bunch of amateurs, to dramatize some idea at your convention. A play or pageant can be good for shock effect, to break monotony, to establish a meeting theme, to help a speaker illustrate a vital point. But don't use drama to say the same thing a speaker will say later. It ruins his speech.

There are firms which specialize in convention theatrics. If you hire one, cut costs on scenery and costumes and props when necessary, but don't stint on talent fees. Be sure you get expert writers, directors, and actors. They make or break your show.

A Better Final Session. Some associations find they're better off without a closing banquet. Their delegates say they'd rather eat where they can table-hop and mingle with everyone they want to meet. Maybe a barbecue or buffet or dance would be the best wind-up for your convention.

If you do have a banquet, how good is your toastmaster? He can be too good. One master of ceremonies kept the crowd laughing for twenty-four minutes, after which an earnest, challenging speaker was a dismal flop. You don't necessarily need a toastmaster at all; it depends on whether the delegates' desire to learn is stronger than their desire to be entertained. If entertainment is necessary, don't follow a funny man with a serious one.

The best-laid plans

Having laid out the broad pattern of your convention, you still need months of preparation to fill in important details. Here are some major items which you and your planning committee might think about.

1. The agenda and the registration lists. Should they be slimmed down? Delegates often complain that a convention has too many people, too many meetings, too many speeches. They ask for shorter speeches and more time for discussion. "A half-hour is long enough for any talk except a real bombshell," some say. Delegates also seem to want more free time for socializing and comparing notes.

2. Advance registration. Convention-scarred chairmen answering a recent questionnaire said almost unanimously that their worst headache was trying to guess how many delegates would attend. Should you plan a prize contest or other device for pulling in registrations well ahead of time?

3. Families. If they're coming, you'll probably want to line up sitters for babies and recreation for the rest of the family. A delegate is in a happier mood if he isn't abandoning wife and kiddies to a lonely hotel room. Left with nothing to do, they're likely to bring pressure for shopping trips, theater excursions and other complicated forays.

A convention with families present has advantages over a stag gathering. The domestic atmosphere helps everyone settle down for serious business sessions. However, there are hazards too. A wife has been known to burn steadily for three days because someone else got a room with a better view.

4. Your speakers. How are you choosing the main attraction? The lazy way is to buy a big name and take what you get. Delegates seeking ideas and information will be cool to a national figure talking broad generalities. However, if it's inspiration they need, a high-powered orator from outside can sometimes bring them to their feet cheering.

Another way of choosing a main speaker is to pick an expert who has sweated out a talk that makes sense. But you'll have to help him do some polishing. Many a shining expert writes a dull speech. He could come up with a brilliant one, if somebody would translate his jargon into plain talk, unravel his outline so it pulls listeners along logically, and make him enrich it with specific examples.

If you pay him a fee you're entitled to insist that he furnish an advance text of his talk long before the convention. Call it a press release if you must. But get it. Then go over it with him, helping him tighten and brighten until you're both sure it's right.

Don't stop there. A good manuscript is only part of the problem. How well will he deliver it? Ideally he shouldn't seem to be reading at all. He should look his audience in the eye, roam around the stage, ram home his points with actions and gestures. Uness he's had considerable platform training, he won't be capable of much of this and there's no use striving for the ideal. But you can go part way anyhow. Get him to tape-record his talk in advance, so he can play it back and improve his diction. Impress on him that a good speaker uses change of pace—fast most of the time but slow for emphasis—and ranges from whisper to shout. Coach him to practice gestures; to smile now and then. He may balk. But you can tactfully remind him that he's the headliner for an important gathering, and that he is to receive an appropriate fee, for which you expect a polished and forceful performance.

Your minor speakers may need help too—as much as you can give. Brief them on the kind of audience they will face; what it knows about the speaker's subject; what it wants to know. (A good starting point for almost any speaker is the assumption that his listeners know little and care little about his subject; that it's up to him to make it interesting and important.)

Who will pay your speakers' travel costs? Sometimes a guest takes it for granted that his hosts, since they've invited him, will defray his expenses. If this isn't to be the case, make it clear in your invitation, and express hope that he'll be in the city at convention time so a trip won't be necessary.

You also should make clear, if his subject is newsworthy,

whether the talk will or won't be off the record. If reporters are invited, he must unavoidably speak for possible publication.

The little things

When you work down to detailed blueprinting of a convention, here are a few fine touches which may help make it a success.

Order a distinctive badge or ribbon for delegates attending for the first time. They'll get extra attention, and will be drawn into conversations more easily.

Brief your section leaders weeks in advance. What manner of people will be in their sections? What will they expect?

Arrange to scatter microphones in the aisles and along the walls, so the audience will be able to ask questions and talk back.

The convention hotel should serve American plan meals, to encourage fraternizing in the dining room. Otherwise delegates will shy from eating in groups, for fear of getting stuck with the check.

Never schedule a golf tourney on the day of a business session. Each ruins the other. You'd be surprised how many men like to join both.

Stack your group meetings carefully. Maybe a group should be balanced between younger and older delegates. Maybe it should include representatives from all types or sizes of chapters. Sometimes the old heads should meet by themselves, free of newer men who might slow them down with kindergarten questions.

Advice to advance men

Life can be beautiful for the man in charge of advance arrangements for a convention—but only if he has prepared well. If he hasn't, here is what may befall him:

He checks in at the hotel a few days before the convention,

and gets his first surprise. The hotel is charging the advance committee the full rate instead of the convention rate. The contract
says nothing about special rates for advance men.

He tries to reach the hotel's sales or convention manager, to
begin checking details. That gentleman is out, or in a meeting.
The office has no idea when he will be available for even a phone
call. "He's a very busy man," says the outer-office sentry.

Hours pass before anyone finds a go-between who can talk
about table arrangements, meeting rooms and sound equipment.
Questions to him produce more surprises. Certain exhibit rooms
and hospitality rooms which you planned to set up in advance
won't be available until the day of the convention. Blackboards
and lecterns are nowhere to be found.

C-day dawns and the convention begins to convene. Delegates
arriving from early planes and trains are told that their rooms will
be available around four p.m. Soon there are long lines of delegates at the room clerks' barricades, glumly waiting to sign the
register and hear how many hours they must wait for the rooms
they reserved. By late afternoon the lobby and bar are jammed
with rumpled, peevish delegates.

A slow trickle of lucky registrants are getting rooms by this
time, but they are handed keys and asked to make their own way
roomward. Luggage will be brought up presently, they are told;
at the moment no bellboy is available. A mountain of suitcases is
piled in the lobby and on the sidewalk.

At nightfall most rooms are more or less ready for occupancy
(which does not necessarily mean that they have been straight-
ened up since departure of previous occupants). In another two
hours bellboys get the luggage delivered.

The second day of the conclave brings more wisdom to the
advance man. He learns what hotel employees think of the convention. They think it's annoying. Doubtless the top management
knows that conventions are a desirable source of income, but the

knowledge hasn't seeped down very far. Delegates are regarded as second-class guests by most of the help, and get short shrift from bellboys and waiters.

Delegates complain that room service is too slow and too costly, that they can't get clean towels, that their rooms aren't made up until evening, that their clothes aren't pressed within forty-eight hours, that washrooms are short of paper. The main meeting room is heated like a crematorium. Round-table rooms aren't heated at all. The movie screen is cracked and torn. Breakfast takes ninety minutes. At the banquet on Friday there isn't enough fish for those who want it. Throughout the day and evening there is a dense crush around the elevators.

The hotel executive who booked the convention is invisible and inaccessible, except when he rebukes the advance man for not releasing unneeded reservations.

The foregoing may not all happen to any one man. But it can, unless he takes precautions which will doubtless have suggested themselves to the reader. Here are additional steps which an advance man may want to take:

Before signing a contract with a hotel:

1. Get references from other groups which have convened there. Check the references.

2. Ask the hotel sales manager what has been done to infuse his own hospitable spirit into other employees. Tactfully convey to him how delegates feel about arrogant room clerks, somnolent bellboys, rude waiters and absentee maids.

3. Make sure he will be available during the convention—or that somebody else with ample authority will be.

4. Ask the sales manager, "What will we sit on?" If he answers "The usual ballroom chair," bid him begone.

(The usual ballroom chair was made for sitting out a dance now and then. It is a torture instrument if used for convention sessions. Many hotels prefer it because it is easy to stack and store. Don't convene at such a hotel unless you can bear to see one-third of your audience steal out early.)

A few weeks before convention time:

1. Arrange to make full use of mimeographs. Check the hotel's mimeographing room.

(Many delegates don't listen continuously, or don't remember. Supply mimeographed reports for everyone to read at leisure. Give out copies of a worth-while speech instead of hoping that listeners will take notes. Instead of oral announcements, send around mimeographed ones.)

2. If the press will cover your convention, make sure of a good press room with typewriters, phones, and other amenities. Get fact sheets ready for newsmen.

3. Decide how to estimate banquet attendance. This is a common headache. In a recent survey 76 per cent of convention authorities admitted that they had been hurt by poor planning of the banquet. Some sort of advance ticket sale or deposit plan is essential. If tickets are sold at the door you're in trouble.

When you arrive for the pre-convention check-up:

1. Go over the menu of each meal. Banquet managers are sometimes carefree about serving ham or bacon without regard to the number of Jewish delegates, and about offering no substitute for meat on Catholic holy days.

2. Personally visit every meeting room. Make sure the seats, acoustics and ventilation are adequate.

(The advance man of one conclave on a college campus thought this precaution was unnecessary, since colleges are accustomed to coping with meetings. When he arrived, he found the main sessions were to be held in the gymnasium, with speakers standing in lonely splendor at the center of the vast floor and the audience sitting in the bleachers at both sidelines. Try this some time and see what happens.)

3. Get on sociable terms with hotel personnel you may need during the convention: the housekeeper, catering manager, bell captain, maintenance staff and others. Learn their names and how to reach them quickly in case of snafu. Some folding money pressed into the right palms may prove a fruitful investment.

The chairman's hot seat

Here are some points a chairman of a convention meeting may want to keep in mind:

Insist on a preview of bulletins, press releases, and announcements. Are your speakers identified so everyone will know who and what they are? Are time and place clear? Is "Open Discussion" appended if you want the audience to talk back?

Post someone to meet your speakers and shepherd them to the right place. If he is to stay overnight, does he know where? Will he need transportation there? Are you following through to make sure he is comfortable after the meeting?

You will need help during a meeting. Your most essential aide, if the program includes speakers, is a timekeeper. By advance agreement with the speaker, the timekeeper must signal unobtrusively when the allotted time is almost up. Keep your program on schedule or be stigmatized as a weak chairman.

You need additional henchmen if your program includes floor discussion. Sometimes an awful silence overcomes the gathering. Avoid fiasco by priming a few friends in the audience.

Another help in an open meeting is to post a summarizer at a blackboard. Beforehand he should write the specific questions to be considered. A blackboard helps to crystallize a rambling discussion, if the summarizer writes each point on the board as a speaker voices it.

If your meeting room is large, you may want hand microphones scattered through it so all who speak can be heard.

A last check of a meeting room is advisable an hour or two before a meeting. You may find that the folding chairs aren't there. You may find that the lights can't be turned on, or the air-conditioning doesn't work, or two groups are scheduled to meet in the same room simultaneously.

Allow yourself more time than you would in a business convention. If this is your first trip to a social work conference you may plan to park your car nearby, only to see too late that there is no parking space within blocks. You may be delayed much longer than you think possible in the hotel dining room. You may find that your meeting has been mysteriously moved elsewhere at the last moment.

One chairman, due to handle a vital section meeting at a big convention, emerged from his room on the sixth floor a good ten minutes before the meeting was to start on the twentieth floor. He supposed he had ample time. But no elevator would stop for him. Every car was jammed and the operators had orders not to pause midway until the rush was over. He reached the twentieth floor very late for his own meeting.

One small difficulty may arise about calling your meeting to order. Many conventioneers have a queer reluctance to enter an assembly room even a minute ahead of time. They loiter just outside the entrance. You need another henchman—a burly, genial one—who can flog them in.

Even if only a handful are present, begin promptly. If you get a reputation as a late starter nobody will come to your sessions on time.

As your first order of business, run through some minor matters while waiting for the crowd to drift in. Once you are well under way, your first duty is to outline the plan for the meeting. Let everyone know whether there may be questions or discussion

—and when. After each talk? When the panel is talked out? After an intermission? (Incidentally, a recess after a talk is an aid to thought.) Should questions be written or vocal? (Most speakers prefer written ones. And so do chairmen, after a few bouts with long-winded interrogators.)

The chairman is *not* expected to make a speech. If he introduces the invited speakers, he should be short. No speaker enjoys a long introduction.

When you preside over discussion, your opinion should never be evident. Stay impartial and unemotional.

When you umpire a hot discussion, you may want to call speakers from opposite sides alternately, and to ask both sides to agree on time limits.

If your speakers are questioned by the audience, your role is middleman. Repeat questions from the floor so everyone hears them. You can rephrase a question to shorten it. You can rule out a question as irrelevant, repetitious, or too broad. You can toss a question to whichever speaker you think should answer it—or even to someone in the audience who is especially well qualified.

Finish on time even if the group wants to continue. Convention committees count on you to keep the agenda on schedule. Even if this is the last meeting of the day, there undoubtedly are delegates who told Bill they'd meet him in the lobby. "Time for one more question," is a chairman's standard way of applying the brakes. Then sum up if you wish, and adjourn. Those who want to stay and talk can do so afterward.

The secret war of the convention bureaus

Where will next year's convention be held? You should realize that many strings will be tugged—some of them invisibly, perhaps —to influence the choice of site.

Important money is at stake. Surveys show that money left in a city by conventioneers during a year can total more than the city's biggest industrial payroll.

Therefore most cities have convention bureaus which push hard and spend heavily. The National Association of Convention Bureaus has a confidential information exchange even though its ninety members compete keenly. Operators from several of these bureaus may be at your convention, maneuvering in the background.

Banners, brochures and "spontaneous" demonstrations for various cities usually indicate that convention bureau men are in your midst. You needn't suppose that mayors or governors drop in through sheer good will to invite the convention to their bailiwicks. It isn't just sentiment which puts those "Next Year Come to Blank City" buttons on hundreds of lapels.

These are only surface manifestations. Even a seasoned conventioneer may not realize what else can be happening out of sight. In order to land a juicy convention for his city, an expert bureau wrangler has been known to engineer a secession movement, split a national organization and form a new one.

One convention bureau overturned an association's national board by inciting a local group to go over the board's head, distribute questionnaires to the rank and file on where they wanted to meet, and evoke the right answers by sending orchids to every convention wife tagged "Blank City would love to entertain you next year."

If the site is to be picked by a committee or by the national board, instead of by vote of the delegates, a city's "lobbyist" will start work months or years ahead. With golf games, quiet dinners, and little gifts he may establish close palship with at least one powerful figure in the inner councils. He may also induce his city's delegates to bore enthusiastically from within at the convention itself. Some of them have the ear of the board.

One convention bureau strategist, seeing that the vote would go against him in the board meeting, invited the opposition members of the board out for an evening on the town 'just to show there's no hard feelings." These members overslept next morning —partly because the hotel switchboard operator was strangely careless about their wake-up calls. They failed to appear at the board meeting, and the lobbyist's city was chosen on a snap vote.

The question of which hotel should be convention headquarters is also inflammable. This hotel normally gets about 70 per cent of the delegates. An average conventioneer spends $60 in his hotel (considerably more than the average tourist).

Scrambling for such a chunk of business can lead to unpleasantness. Overnight, one governing board voted to take the selection of the hotel out of the hands of a special committee as a result of bribery charges.

All of which means merely that the choice of site should be made coolly and cautiously, with proper precautions. Forewarned is forearmed.

After you've gone

Here are some random notes which may help you tie up loose ends:

You may think you will remember what was said at those important meetings and conversations—but you won't. Round out your notes quickly, before it is too late.

A common complaint of conventioneers is that there is no follow-up of their resolutions and recommendations. Have you a plan for implementing the convention's decisions?

Many conventions and conferences in the welfare world are held at camps. If yours is, make sure to leave the camp in as good or better shape than you found it.

If you made worth-while contacts at the convention, you will want to consolidate them with a letter afterward—and maybe a card at Christmas.

How about the people who helped with your part of the convention? Were your thank-you letters obvious form letters, or were they specific enough so each man could see you appreciated his particular job? Did your ghost-writer get a courtesy copy of the speech as finally delivered, or is he still wondering whether most of it was junked? Did all the people in that group photo get prints? Did the fellow who made a suggestion get a grateful note (with copy to his associates) telling him his suggestion was adopted? Did your publicity chairman ever see the clippings that his work produced (and does he know that you saw them)? Did your hosts in the community and the hotel feel cordial toward you when you left? Did you leave tips for every employee who should be tipped?

CHAPTER 19

A Few Thousand Last Words

Time to quit?

So YOU'VE DECIDED to give up your unpaid job.

Why?

Surely not because you're too old. Happily, there is no retirement age in community service. The many worlds of civic work are teeming with white-haired chairmen, committeemen, presidents, ministers, even athletic coaches—still having as much fun as Santa Claus, long past the year when corporate regulations would condemn them to the shelf. If you decide you've slowed down too much for the all-round job you've been doing, use your head instead of your legs. Deputize other people for the heavy roadwork. You can still transmit high-voltage enthusiasm and insight and ideas from a wheel chair if necessary, as football coach Knute Rockne did before his death—or even by phone, as plus-seventy Henry Kaiser does when he can't plunge personally into the hubbub.

Maybe you want to quit because the work has gone badly of late. Perhaps rival groups have outshone yours. Your organization isn't the super-duper all-conquering team it should be.

Before you resign for this reason, ponder the words of Hal Stebbins, an aging but still-active adman and civic benefactor: "You are remembered for the hand and heart you held out to those on the way up. When you get to the pearly gates, St. Peter isn't going to ask, 'Were you in the Top Ten?' He is more likely to ask, 'What did you do to help the Bottom Ten?' "

If you're helping other people, defeats and failures shouldn't stop you. Look back over the steep trail you've climbed. Look at the load you've carried. Remember the high spots instead of the low—the value of your burden, not the soreness of your feet. Take a sharp look at—and laugh at—your own itch for triumphs and recognition; you didn't go into civic work to butter your ego. Hark back to the thrill you got from knowing that somebody benefited from work you did. Recall how it feels to bounce out of bed with a mind full of plans and a body boiling with energy for a challenging task. You can recapture that mood by remembering it and the achievements it produced.

After twenty-five years of studying the subject, Dr. Rexford Hersey of the University of Pennsylvania says that virtually everyone gets a what's-the-use mood at intervals as regular as the tide and the calendar. Be prepared for yours. Don't let them get you down.

But perhaps instead of feeling blue you're seeing red. You've been flouted, tricked, outvoted, insulted, thwarted.

This may be cause to resign. Or it may not. Remember Monsignor Fulton J. Sheen's adage, "When you're getting kicked in the rear, it means you're in front."

Theodore F. MacManus pointed out in *The Penalty of Leadership:* "In every field of human endeavor, he that is first must perpetually live in the white light of publicity. . . . The reward is widespread recognition; the punishment, fierce denial and detraction. When a man's work becomes a standard, it also becomes a target for the shafts of the envious few. If his work be merely mediocre, he will be left severely alone—if he achieve a masterpiece, it will set a million tongues wagging."

Never mind if your hair is on fire and your back is full of

buckshot. Put away that meat-ax. Go take a bath and a brief vacation. Look up a classic psychological study by a group of Yale
scientists, *Frustration and Aggression.* It points out that whenever
we are blocked by somebody or something, we begin to feel pent
up and irritated. Then we do something rash. This is normal. But
if we realize what goes on inside us, we can save everybody a
good deal of needless storm and strife.

The best way to handle that frustrated fury is to channel its
energy into hard, useful work—preferably work which finds a
physical outlet. Grab a spade and dig madly in your garden. Rip
into the filing or typing or repair work you've been putting off.
Meanwhile, postpone quitting your civic job until you've had
plenty of time to consider alternatives. There may be more adroit
strategies for coping with the troublemakers who infuriate you.
Let's consider a few in the next section.

Local villain makes good

Occasionally the best way of dealing with trouble is to ignore
it. "It is no inconsiderable part of wisdom to know how much
of an evil ought to be tolerated," said Burke. Perhaps you've been
upset by something that won't seem so horrendous a month from
now.

In one town, the hard-working chairman of the convention
committee of the Chamber of Commerce was beset by critics
within his own committee. At a meeting of the board of directors
they openly flayed him. His blunders, his neglect, his indecision
were villainous, they said. He knew they were magnifying minor
flaws and attacking him unjustly. But he sat silent. When they
finished, and the board turned to him expecting an angry rebuttal,
he merely said quietly, "I have nothing to say."

Some of the carpers blushed. They suddenly remembered all
the good work he had done without praise. In the silence that

followed, their high-pitched indictment echoed tinnily. Finally the board chairman said, "Most of us know what our convention chairman has done for this organization over the years. I don't think he needs any defense. The previous remarks were out of order, so we'll move on to the next item of business if there is no objection." There was none.

Another strategy when you're a target of internal sniping is to set up worth-while new goals which excite the organization. Maybe your group has become stagnant, leaving idle hands and idle tongues to make mischief. The noted American sociologist, Samuel A. Stouffer, studied American soldiers in wartime and found them full of frustrations, due to sudden loss of civilian freedom. They needled the brass in devious ways, often most unfairly. But in combat, soldiers felt far more fraternal toward their officers—because they could "discharge their aggression directly against the enemy."

Of course another move—always an essential one—is to step back and see how you look from the viewpoint of your critics. Maybe a compromise, or an explanation, or even a forthright reversal of your stand will be indicated when you re-examine the situation calmly. Only mules and milestones never change their minds.

On the back of an envelope found among his effects after his death, former Atomic Energy Commission Chairman Gordon Dean had jotted a set of "Lessons Learned." Among them were:

In a pinch always first assume that a man is good and that at worst he is in the gray area between good and bad.

The greatest builder of confidence is the ability to do something—almost anything—well. When that confidence comes, strive for humility; you aren't as good as all that.

The way to become truly useful is to seek the best that other brains have to offer. Use them to supplement your own, and give credit to them.

The greatest tragedies stem from misunderstandings. Answer: Communicate.

You probably remember the story of the revolutionary leader who was sitting in a café when a crowd charged past. He jumped up. Someone asked where he was going. "I'm not sure," he answered, "but I must get in front, for I'm their leader."

If you are a leader, you too may sometimes face this embarrassment. You may not be leading your followers where they want to go. Should you get in front, and show them the way to their goal? Or try to divert them to another goal? Or forsake them? Depending on the goals and the circumstances, sometimes one choice is wisest, sometimes another.

Don't be sad because you feel isolated from your followers. Good leaders are often lonely. Dr. Herbert C. Modlin of the Menninger Foundation tells of his own experience: "I became aware that one of our group was moving, and several other members of the team had gone over to help. No one had said anything to me about it. Nobody had asked me to help. I was telling my superior about this and wryly said, 'They left me out; they rejected me.'

"He said, 'Congratulations! You are really the team leader now.'"

Leaders must also watch themselves, in time of stress, for what Victoria Lincoln calls "the lust for martyrdom that drives many to reject all tact, all gradualism in their hungry embrace of unpopular causes." Sometimes we think we're making a heroic stand on principle when we're just stubborn, angry, and self-pitying. Instead of martyrdom, would diplomacy serve the organization better in the long run?

Yet when all this is said and weighed, we must recognize that there are times when it's best to quit. Work which once was interesting can become boring. Sometimes you are side-tracked into a position where you have no work worth doing. And sometimes there is a basic, unavoidable collision of personalities or principles. If you can't win it, you should get out.

One Scoutmaster in Chaos Falls, New York, found himself in conflict with vestrymen of the church which sponsored his troop. He taught a Sunday School class there. The troop had started in his class, but grew to include almost every boy of Scout age in the parish. His troop took week-end camping trips once a month. On Sunday mornings when the troop was away, the boys' side of Sunday school was almost empty. Naturally the vestrymen objected.

The Scoutmaster argued, "I conduct chapel services on Sunday mornings in camp. Our boys get as much religious instruction there as they do in Sunday School." The church men were unconvinced.

The troop's regular Tuesday night meetings were held in the Sunday School room. When a new carpet was laid there, the vestry decreed that the troop must meet outdoors on the basketball court except on rainy nights. This led to more wrangling between Scoutmaster and vestry.

The breaking point came when the vestry discovered that six of the troop's fifty boys came from families not connected with the church. "Why should this church make its facilities available to boys for whom it has no responsibility?" the vestrymen demanded.

"Boys make friends outside the church," the Scoutmaster retorted. "They enjoy belonging to an organization—such as a Scout troop—to which their friends belong." The empurpled vestrymen laid down the law: No troop activities on Sunday. No troop meetings in the Sunday School room. No boys in the troop who were not in the Sunday School.

The Scoutmaster saw this was the end of the road. He resigned. Pleased with such a prompt solution, the vestry made only token efforts to replace him. The troop disbanded. This solution wasn't so pleasing to the boys, or to some of their parents. Within a month nearly every Scout had joined troops sponsored by other churches; and many of them switched Sunday Schools too.

Human nature being what it is, the ex-Scoutmaster inwardly guffawed when some of the vestrymen asked him to reorganize the troop on his own terms. Once again, a local villain had been vindicated. However, he knew he would be unwise to try to work further with the same men who had fought him so fiercely. Instead he accepted leadership of a troop of slum kids sponsored by his service club. The Sunday School room had few boys on its fine carpet for years afterward.

Break clean, or fade away?

General MacArthur's famous remark that old soldiers just fade away is sometimes a good guide for worn-out civic workers. On the other hand, a clean break is more often the best course.

The fadeaway is indicated when you want to shift your load gradually, or when you want to ease out of an unpleasant situation without stirring up further unpleasantness.

For example, a leader who has built up an organization by the force and skill of his own leadership might wreck it by resigning openly. Even if he announced his departure long in advance, allowing plenty of time for replacements to be trained, gloom might reign. Prospective replacements might be paralyzed at the prospect of trying to fill his shoes. Recruitment might dwindle.

How much better off his organization would be if he could manage to edge his way offstage a little at a time! He might announce that some temporary condition of health or business would force him to give less attention to the organization for the next month or two. He could arrange for assistants to take over part, but not all, of his duties "for the time being." Then he could absent himself longer and oftener, still keeping an eye on operations, giving his assistants coaching when they needed it, letting everyone gradually get used to functioning without him.

This same gentle tactic is useful for a volunteer committeeman or board member who finds he can't work peaceably with his colleagues. If he should suddenly resign, on whatever excuse, they might see through it. His "blowup" with others in the organization might be widely discussed. Of course if others are depending on him to carry out certain tasks, he must carry them out or get somebody else to. But he need not say he is quitting. He can arrange for a temporary leave of absence; then reappear for a while but avoid taking new responsibilities. In time he will be able to resign quietly, leaving no ripples.

The beauty of this method is that it allows you leeway to change your mind if conditions change, or if you find that you miss the people and the work more woefully than you thought you would. Many an active volunteer has found an unexpected, aching void in his life when the phone stops ringing, there are no meetings to attend, nobody needs him.

But the clear, explicit resignation is usually a better way to break off. It leaves nobody wondering whether you can or cannot be counted on in future. When it is the result of disagreement, it makes plain to everyone that there *was* disagreement; this may produce healthy changes, or at least second thoughts, within the group. Your friction or frustration, if stated with dignity and without heat, may make everyone see how to make conditions happier for your successor.

If you are leaving because of boredom, you can say this tactfully. It may teach the organization to pick a replacement who has different interests than yours. Or it may insure that the next man will be given more challenging work.

Of course you can proffer a resignation as a bluff, to wring concessions from those who oppose you. If you plan it this way, you'll want to brace yourself for a rude shock in case it doesn't work. Resignations are accepted far oftener than not. A man may be Mr. Indispensable in his own eyes, only to find that others would rather struggle along without him than kneel and beg him to continue.

When you face the firing squad

Once in a great while a man makes an involuntary exit from a community organization. His critics decide he must go. Without warning, and usually without explanation, he finds himself on the outside.

On one long-remembered evening in San Diablo, a hospital held its annual banquet and installation of board members without telling six men they were being dropped from the board. They attended with their wives, expecting to be automatically re-elected as they had been for years past.

In another case in the same town, a troop committee abruptly phoned its Scoutmaster to serve notice that it had decided not to reappoint him, and that another man was taking his place that same evening. Not surprisingly, this was a committee which had secretly contrived the ouster of its own chairman a year previously.

Such crude power politicking eventually ruins an organization. Everybody in it begins to wonder if he will be the next victim of its plots and purges. And people outside feel contemptuous of the cheap little clique in control.

But the approaching downfall of the cabal may be small satisfaction to you, if you happen to be on the receiving end of the bum's rush. Even a suave and smooth ejection is hard to accept gracefully. Nobody enjoys discovering he is not wanted, especially if he has rendered services which deserve gratitude. Perhaps you can admit to yourself, after you cool off, that someone else will render better service than you can; but your first impulse will probably be to hit back.

Of course this is almost always a mistake. You seldom gain anything by bickering with the people who pushed you out. Certainly you won't want to work further with them. And while you may (or may not) gain sympathy if you call attention to the rough treatment you've received, why bother? You don't need sympathy, do you? Nor do you need the childish satisfaction of avenging yourself on petty persecutors.

Now and then someone manages to face the firing squad with good humor as well as dignity. One of the trustees who was dropped from the San Diablo board asked permission to attend one more board meeting. The board could scarcely say no. At the meeting, he told the trustees: "That last election rather took me by surprise. I expected to be working with you this year, helping complete some of the projects we started together. But as I look around and see the new members you've elected, I admit that the new board will accomplish more than the old board could. On the board or off, I'm still interested in the hospital. My means are limited, but I want to give you my check for twenty-five dollars toward the equipment of the building we completed last year, and to assure you that I'll always be glad to help personally whenever you need my particular abilities."

It was a sincere and generous gesture, but it produced some red faces on the board, and the ex-trustee may be forgiven for noting this with quiet amusement.

Similarly, the young Scoutmaster rose above his humiliation when the San Diablo troop committee discharged him. "I'm sorry I disappointed you as a leader," he said, "but you know better than I what kind of leader you want for your boys. For my own good, though, I'd appreciate your telling me frankly where I fell down. I don't want to go on making the same mistakes."

The committee thereupon gave him some fatherly advice, so

the final parting was friendly. He profited from the advice, and became a successful leader of another troop.

In Chaos Falls a committee chairman in a service club discovered that members of his own committee were meeting secretly to plot his removal. He counterattacked frontally. Calling his committee together, he asked about their secret meetings. "Give it to me straight, boys. Should I resign as chairman? What's behind this?"

The committeemen mumbled and hung their heads, but the ringleader spoke out. "We know you don't agree with our ideas. We want those ideas carried out. That means we need a new chairman."

"Okay," said the chairman. "We differ, but that's no cause for hard feelings. Suppose we ask the president to dissolve the whole committee and lay both points of view before the club. He can explain them without any of us publicly taking sides. Then he can appoint a new committee to do whatever the club wants."

The chairman didn't feel he was fighting for his job. He realized that the real fight was not against him, but against a policy. He made sure that the issue would be decided by the whole club, as was fitting, rather than by a small group inside the committee. Thus he forestalled a bitter personal set-to. (As luck would have it, the club membership supported his viewpoint, and the president reappointed him with a new committee which could support him heartily.)

Exit smiling

George Washington, being the father of his country, was able to make a farewell address that deeply moved everyone. Other men are seldom as effective when attempting a valedictory speech. As you bow out, you may do well to decide with Tennyson,

. . . . may there be no sadness of farewell
When I embark.

If the organization chooses to bestow gifts and eulogies on you, well and good. But words of wisdom from you will only make the audience fidget. Even at a testimonial dinner, the best farewell address is likely to be, "Thank you, my friends. It has been a pleasure to work with you. Good night."

As you leave, you'll be looking around for some other organization to serve, we hope. There are countless worthy causes which need manpower. And any man of good will feels an inner need to be doing something for other people, right up to the end of his life. Group work is a great cure for loneliness and other ills which beset us in later years. A noted physician and psychologist, Dr. Harry Levinson, says, "For mental health and balance, invest one's self in other people. In prescribing a course of treatment we often suggest that people take on some kind of voluntary work where they as individuals are critically important in the lives of somebody else."

As a final word, then, it seems fitting to emphasize the points made in the beginning of this book. You were invited to help build your community because your ability and spirit were recognized. When you accepted, you put your reputation on the line. It is to be hoped that you gave something more than the luster of your name or a reluctant financial contribution. Your business skills, and the lifting power of your own personality, are the real contributions which you should have made—and probably did, or you wouldn't have read thus far in this book.

Now, as you retire from one frontier of community work, you have built up an equity. Intangible dividends will be coming in for years. You'll get deep satisfaction from watching the seeds you planted grow and flourish. You'll never lose the friends you've made.

No doubt there have been headaches and heartaches. But isn't it true that we really learn only from experiences which touch us emotionally—either with pleasure or pain? And that the more intense the emotion, the more vividly the lesson is etched in memory? That's why most of us have long forgotten most of the information which was force-fed us at school, but have always remembered the valuable and hard-won lessons we learned in community work. We're all better and wiser men for the services we've tried to render.

So on this day of retirement, you can look back serenely on opponents as well as allies. They were a fine crew to work with. It *was* a pleasure to work with them. Let your final handshake be warm and friendly. Go with a grin. And, as the Spanish say, go with God.